'The book of Numbers is all too easily overloo~~~~ ~~
even though it recounts the things t'~~~~~~~~
to serve as an example, and ... w~~~~~~
(1 Corinthians 10:11). This Lent de~~~~~
the Israelites on their journey throug~~~~~
examples and instructions, offering u~~~~~~~~ ~~~ng us to do
better as we face our own wilderness ex~~~~~~~nces today.'
Dr Ros Clarke, Associate Director of Church Society

'Warm, honest, inviting biblical wisdom. Mark is a thoughtful, relaxed, guide as we journey through the book of Numbers, always helping us see how the story of God's people in the wilderness is taken up in Jesus' own life and, through the New Testament, in our own lives. A model in the use of the Old Testament in the life of Jesus' disciples today.'
The Revd Professor Jeremy Duff, Principal of St Padarn's Theological Institute

'During Lent, we often talk about the wilderness but rarely take time to reflect on the story of God's people in the wilderness that is laid out in Numbers. This brilliant book of reflections takes us step by step through the book of Numbers and opens our eyes to the many riches that wilderness experiences can offer. I highly recommend it!'
Dr Paula Gooder, writer and speaker

'In the wake of the personal and societal wilderness brought on by the COVID-19 pandemic, this Lenten devotional is especially fitting for a time such as this. Mark skilfully approaches Numbers, a book whose pages are often intentionally passed over, and makes it wonderfully accessible in a way not seen often. His balance of interesting historical background, modern cultural references and relatable personal anecdotes helps to illustrate and illuminate the story of God's character and his faithfulness to his people Israel even among the trials of their wilderness wanderings on the way to the Promised Land. More importantly, throughout this devotional Mark ties the Lord's promises to Israel with his ultimate plan for all the nations in the sending of his son Jesus Christ for the redemption of the whole world!'
Canon Wes Jagoe, Canon to the Archbishop of the Anglican Church in North America

'Mark Broadway offers everything that should be in a good Lenten study book. It doesn't need any specialist prior knowledge at all – Mark does not browbeat with theology, but provides straightforward, grounded daily theological insight relevant to our modern lives. For many of us, Numbers has been literally and metaphorically a "closed book" of the Bible. But here it is opened to us with deft skill, as Mark draws us into the dramatic narrative and calls our attention to the constant points of reference between our own lives and these ancient events. In doing so, he imbues them with an engaging freshness: this is personal Bible study at its best. It is written for absolutely everyone, though I wonder – with some professional excitement – if this is a Bible study guide which will be rather more accessible to men than is typical for the genre, and only in part because of the nature of the events described in Numbers. I can recommend this book gladly, and will be buying copies for friends.'
Canon Tim Llewellyn Jones, Director of Ministry and Discipleship, Llandaff Diocese

'In this delightful study, Mark does three very helpful things. First, he offers us a positive and manageable way into the book of Numbers, which is both a vital part of the canon and a neglected one. Second, he makes creative and insightful connections with other parts of Scripture. Third, he connects both of these with the realities of the lived Christian life, drawing from his own experience and insight. The combination is certain to be an encouragement and a blessing for your Lenten journey. Take and read!'
The Revd Dr Ian Paul, theologian, author and speaker

JOURNEYING WITH GOD
IN THE WILDERNESS

Mark Broadway is an Anglican priest in the diocese of Llandaff, south Wales. Prior to ordination, Mark moved to Wales where he studied legal practice at postgraduate level before later obtaining his MTh in theology and beginning his ministry. Since taking up his most recent post, Mark has trained as a volunteer crew member at his local Royal National Lifeboat Institute (RNLI) station and has served as a Covid chaplain at his local hospital. Mark writes from his own perspective, which has been shaped as much by his experience of life as it has been by his learning.

JOURNEYING WITH GOD IN THE WILDERNESS

A forty-day Lent devotional
through the book of Numbers

Mark Broadway

INTER-VARSITY PRESS
SPCK Group, Studio 101, The Record Hall, 16–16A Baldwin's Gardens, London EC1N 7RJ,
England
Email: ivp@ivpbooks.com
Website: www.ivpbooks.com

First published 2023

British Library Cataloguing-in-Publication Data
A catalogue record for this book is available from the British Library.

ISBN: 978-1-78974-465-1
eBook ISBN: 978-1-78974-466-8

Set in Minion Pro 9.75/12.25pt
Typeset in Great Britain by CRB Associates, Potterhanworth, Lincolnshire
Printed and bound in Great Britain by Clays Ltd, Elcograf S.p.A.

Produced on paper from sustainable sources

*Inter-Varsity Press publishes Christian books that are true to the Bible and that
communicate the gospel, develop discipleship and strengthen the church for
its mission in the world.*

*IVP originated within the Inter-Varsity Fellowship, now the Universities and Colleges
Christian Fellowship, a student movement connecting Christian Unions in universities and
colleges throughout Great Britain, and a member movement of the International Fellowship
of Evangelical Students. Website: www.uccf.org.uk. That historic association is maintained,
and all senior IVP staff and committee members subscribe to the UCCF Basis of Faith.*

For all those who find themselves in the wilderness:
may you find streams in the desert
and hear the voice that would speak kindly to you.

Contents

Acknowledgements

This is not a scholarly work. If I were equipped to write a scholarly work, it would not be on the book of Numbers. What I do offer is a pastoral reflection indebted to the scholarly endeavours of others. To understand something of the world of Numbers, I leaned upon the work of experts in the book of Numbers, most notably Gordon Wenham and Dennis T. Olson, as well as others in the field of Old Testament studies such as Christopher Wright. It was necessary also to utilise the work of those who could provide a broader view of Biblical Studies, not least Ian Paul. Ian's insights and encouragement, both in person and in his Tyndale Commentary on the book of Revelation, helped to crystallise my approach to reading Numbers. I am grateful for the opportunity and freedom to write which has been afforded to me by my clerical colleagues who have kept me busy enough that I haven't been bored, but not so busy that I couldn't write. And finally, to those friends who have been kind enough to tell me where I am wrong – which is an almost unending task.

Introduction

Beginnings

The year 2020 marked the beginning of a wilderness journey for many of us. This book seeks to make sense of the wilderness experiences of God's people in order to inform how we think about our own experiences of the wilderness.

In the summer of 2020, I was arranging a funeral and working with the bereaved family. The widow turned to me, saying 'Father', and after I realised she was speaking to me as a priest, rather than looking for her own dad, I met her gaze as she continued, 'Do you think God sent coronavirus?' It is hard to answer such questions without causing more harm than good. On the one hand, I wanted to avoid any notion that God was *directly* responsible; but at the same time, I was reticent to imply that the world was spinning out of control, released from God's care. 'It is a matter of perspective,' I ventured. From a natural perspective, the virus came from a chain of natural causes. Nothing to see here. But the more interesting perspective, for me at least, is the eternal perspective. In the light of eternity (that is to say, in the light of our belief in God), what good might have been found in the midst of the suffering?

Or, to put it another way: looking back from the promised land, what lessons might we have learned in the wilderness?

It makes sense for so many of us to use that language of journeying through a wilderness to describe our lives during the lockdowns that characterised the pandemic or during the stresses of Brexit, or to describe living through the Russian invasion of Ukraine. It has been a wilderness of social isolation and exclusion, of loneliness and frustration. For lots of us, the pandemic was the first extended taste of how life is for so many people around the world who suffer from various chronic illnesses, or who find themselves subject to systemic injustice, exclusion or oppression. One friend of mine who suffers from chronic anxiety remarked to me how her years of experience dealing with her illness had helped her to prepare for and manage her response to Covid and the various lockdowns. In fact, she said, this enabled her to help others who did not have the same hard-won resilience.

I am not one to over-spiritualise such experiences. I try not to force such a lens upon the experience of another. Nevertheless, I can see how it is often possible to look back with the benefit of hindsight and to apply new layers of meaning to the difficulty that has been lived through or endured. This has been true for me and I believe that this can also be true for anyone.

Writing in 1843, the Danish philosopher Søren Kierkegaard said: 'Life can only be understood backwards; but it must be lived forwards.'[1] This rings true for most of us. It is also true of the wilderness narratives which the Bible has recorded for us. We find these wilderness narratives in the book of Numbers, but also in the story of Abraham, Sarah and their family, in the accounts of King David, the Prophet Elijah and many others. They read best as the reflections of a people who have survived, or even flourished, in the wilderness – not as simple travelogue journals. Indeed, one reason why I feel we are able to make assessments of our own lives, and retrospectively to see the hand of God at work, is because of the great multitude of wilderness literature that the Bible affords us. Ancient stories of survival inform our current experiences of grief and distress. Narratives can shape the way in which we respond to the circumstances that we find ourselves enduring – they are literature through which God speaks to us in the wilderness.

The wilderness

Although it is often said that we should not 'judge a book by its cover', it is hard not to judge a book by its title. Perhaps you judged this book by its title!

The English title for the book of the Bible that we will be exploring is 'Numbers'. It is a straightforward translation of the title given in the Greek version of the Hebrew Scriptures, the Septuagint. This was *Arithmoi*, meaning literally 'Numbers' – the same root word from which the English term *arithmetic* is derived. The title given in the Hebrew text is different, however. There the book is called *Bemidbar* meaning 'In the Wilderness'.[2]

---

1 S. Kierkegaard, *Kierkegaard's Journals and Notebooks*, vol. 2, *Journals EE–KK*, ed. by Bruce H. Kirmmse et al. (Princeton, NJ: Princeton University Press, 2008), JJ.167 (1843), p. 179.

2 G. Wenham, *Numbers,* Tyndale Old Testament Commentaries 4 (Nottingham: Inter-Varsity Press, 2008), p. 15.

These two different titles may well give rise to two different sets of presuppositions about what the book contains.

It's easy to see how the English and Greek epithet came to be. It was almost certainly inspired by the two major censuses that dominate chapters 1 to 4 and 26.[3] In those sections of the account, the book of Numbers tells us how the people of Israel were counted and enlisted into service. In his classic commentary on Numbers, Gordon Wenham is at pains not to let any modern aversion to numbers, which may be thought of along with the dreaded word 'statistics', create a false image in our minds of the content of the book.

It might be that you, like me, struggled with maths in school; and so think of numbers and those sort of things as cold and dehumanising. I am not sure that is always the case in the modern world. During the height of the coronavirus pandemic, it was widely reported that millions of people were tuning into the Daily Briefing, which was given by the UK Government. On the surface, this appeared to be a broadcast all about numbers and statistics; it was stocked with charts and graphs, and so many of us listened intently to numbers that we knew represented real people, real lives and tragically real deaths. Likewise, in the ancient world, numbers were understood to be powerful in their ability to convey significance and meaning. Even so, it is a mistake to think that these two census segments are typical of the whole of the book. Although they do play an important role in the story of God's people, the census portions of the text do not represent the depth and breadth of ideas and narrative contained within, and transmitted by, the stories of this book.

The Hebrew title given to this book, *Bemidbar*, meaning 'In the Wilderness' or more simply 'The Wilderness', comes from the fifth (or first distinctive) word of the book. It is the incipit of both the book as a whole and of the first portion of the book as it is appointed to be read in synagogues. An incipit is the word used to denote the start of a piece of music, a reading or a prayer. Figuratively, it sets the tone. This title, *The Wilderness*, locates the beginning of the story in the wilderness of Sinai. This is the first piece of land between the two geographical bookends that demarcate the physical and chronological space that this book deals with. First, to the south and west, the Red Sea with its flight from slavery in

---

3   Wenham, *Numbers*, p. 15.

3

Egypt. Then, to the east and north, the Jordan, with its crossing to the promised land that materialises in the later book, Joshua.

This title, *The Wilderness*, sets the scene. 'Wilderness' calls to mind both the geographical reality that surrounded the people of God, and also the spiritual reality that was redeemed and eventually overcome by the presence of God. More than this, the wilderness becomes, according to the Prophet Hosea, the place of simplicity where God can woo his people. Taking *The Wilderness* as a title prepares the reader to trace the wilderness existence of God's people as they prepare to enter and take hold of the promised land. There are, of course, setbacks along the way – but these setbacks become the context into which God speaks. In God's mercy, failures become the occasion for grace, and Israel's rebellions become the scene in which God's presence is made known. Indeed, although we might be able to see the setbacks, and frequent looking back, of God's people as characteristic and indicative of the natural state of the human heart – sick with sin, and full of desire to return to the slavery of Egypt – nevertheless, in this place of wilderness, God is made known.

Through all the ups and downs of this wilderness adventure, we join with God's people as they learn to see the sure and certain fulfilment of God's future promises. Not to mention God's abiding presence through, as well as in, the wilderness.

Lent

Every year, many Christians make space for the wilderness. In fact, seeking out a wilderness experience has been part of what it has meant to be a Christian for more than a millennium. In one sense, there were the desert fathers and mothers. These were monastic saints, who sought to flee from the pressures and temptations of the city, or civilisation more broadly, to live a holy life in the wilderness. Many of these saints sought refuge in the wilderness, knowing from the Bible how God had always been with his people in the dry and difficult places in which they had sojourned.

Anthony the Great is perhaps the most well known of these ascetics, thanks to the biography of his life and ministry written by Athanasius of Alexandria. It is understood that around the year AD 270 he retreated into the desert, fleeing the pleasures of life which he held to be a corrupting influence. Some years later, he emerged from his isolation and dedicated about five years to the disciples who had begun to congregate around him.

This sort of wilderness experience was never going to be possible for every Christian. Fortunately, the Church had developed a way of bringing the wilderness experience into the life and rhythm of the liturgical year – this was Lent. Of course, not every Christian has called Lent by this name. The English word *Lent* comes from the Anglo-Saxon term for spring, in a similar way to how the English word *Easter* grew out of the Anglo-Saxon month in which the festival usually fell. Most Christians, either currently or throughout history, have not been English speakers. It is helpful to recognise that, in other languages, the season of Lent is usually designated by a word that means something like either 'fasting time' or 'forty'.

Lent is a period of forty fasting days, punctuated by six Sunday feast days, so that even in the midst of the Lenten wilderness there are springs of grace – much like the water from the rock in Numbers 20. The forty days of Lent are full of powerful significance. It is widely known that they point towards the forty days that Jesus spent fasting in the wilderness, an episode that you can find in Matthew 4:1–11. But forty days is a significant amount of time throughout the Bible. We probably all remember from Sunday school that the rain fell for forty days and forty nights in the story of Noah's Flood (Genesis 7:4), but it may have passed us by that Noah waited on top of the mountain for forty days before releasing the raven. Significantly for us, there are various periods of 'forty' spent in the wilderness, to which we will return later.

The Lenten reflections contained in this book seek to search out the lessons that the people of Israel learned through their long sojourn, and so equip us with the resources that we each need to make fuller sense of our own wilderness experiences in the light of eternity. More often than not, as we will see, the ancient Israelites learned these lessons the hard way. This is all the more reason for us to cherish the record of their experience, and not to suffer the same pains ourselves. As we emulate something of Jesus' time in the wilderness during Lent, we are also reaching further back into the story of God and his people. We are leaning into and living something of the wilderness experiences of the people of Israel.

Every reflection, one for each of the forty days of Lent (thus excluding Sundays), will draw upon the wisdom of the book of Numbers as a form of wilderness literature. The flow of the narrative will be followed in part, but the thrust of each reflection will seek to pierce through to find a meaning within the narrative; a meaning which can be both native to the text and also lively and relevant for us.

Mark Broadway

Part 1

REVELATION AT SINAI (NUMBERS 1:1 – 10:10)
A. The preparation (Numbers 1:1 – 4:49)

The opening chapters of Numbers find the people of God encamped below Mount Sinai where they received the law of God – as detailed in the preceding books, Leviticus and Exodus. The time elapsed since the events of the exodus has been approximately one year. During this time, God's people have been journeying. This journey has been spiritual as much as physical, as the people have slowly acclimatised to their departure from slavery in Egypt. Now, as Numbers opens, Moses readies the Israelites for their journey across the wilderness. First, they must be counted and enlisted into service, before they are equipped with new laws and new promises.

The first four days of Lent
Ash Wednesday: be prepared (Numbers 1:1–3)
Thursday: fire (Numbers 2:1–2, 17)
Friday: substitution (Numbers 3:40–3)
Saturday: body (Numbers 4:4–6, 15)

1

Be prepared

The LORD spoke to Moses in the wilderness of Sinai, in the tent of meeting, on the first day of the second month, in the second year after they had come out of the land of Egypt, saying: Take a census of the whole congregation of Israelites, in their clans, by ancestral houses, according to the number of names, every male individually; from twenty years old and upwards, everyone in Israel able to go to war. You and Aaron shall enrol them, company by company.
(Numbers 1:1–3)

Jesus said: 'Or what king, going out to wage war against another king, will not sit down first and consider whether he is able with ten thousand to oppose the one who comes against him with twenty thousand? If he cannot, then, while the other is still far away, he sends a delegation and asks for the terms of peace.'
(Luke 14:31–2)

When preparing to take my two young sons on a nature walk, careful preparation is essential. Spare socks, a large fresh drink and plenty of snacks to be eaten prior to the ubiquitous jam sandwiches which have pride of place at the midway picnic. Although our hikes last only a few hours, it is vital for everything to be properly prepared. Our reading from the book of Numbers opens with detailed preparation. The Israelites are to march to, enter and seize the promised land; but in order for them to do so, they must be prepared. In a similar vein, Jesus says that those who wish to become his disciples must be prepared. They must *count the cost* and determine whether they have the resources. Mercifully, when we discover that we are not prepared, and that we do not have the resources, God supplies grace.

The combination of Shrove Tuesday and Ash Wednesday is unique in that these days are something of a double preparation.

First, they help to prepare us for the coming season of Lent. We might think of pancake day, or *Mardi gras,* as an excuse to party (perhaps it is that!), but it is not *only* that. Using up of sweet treats and ingredients prior to the Lenten fast is also a matter of removing temptation. A custom developed prior to the advent of perpetually stocked supermarkets, eating everything first was a sure-fire way of reducing the urge to snack during Lent. But Shrove Tuesday is more focused than this. Our word *shrove* is derived from a word meaning 'absolution', and is tied tightly to the practice of confessing sins. The confession of sins can be thought of as putting down heavy weights, things that we do not need to carry. It is the loosing of bonds, which Jesus would have us freed from. This comes to something of a climax on Ash Wednesday, either in the form of ashing, as is common among many churches; or in the distinctively Anglican service of Commination, which offers these words:

> Let us therefore return unto him, who is the merciful receiver of all true penitent sinners; assuring ourselves that he is ready to receive us, and most willing to pardon us, if we come unto him with faithful repentance; if we submit ourselves unto him, and from henceforth walk in his ways; if we will take his easy yoke and light burden upon us, to follow him in lowliness, patience, and charity, and be ordered by the governance of his Holy Spirit.
> (Book of Common Prayer, A Commination)

The second layer of preparation is that Lent itself is a season of preparation. If we have prepared ourselves for Lent, it is so that, through our Lenten observances, we might prepare ourselves for Easter. Some customs and traditions in church life help to reflect this aim. For example, the putting away of decorations, even veiling images and statues that normally brighten the church building, is to create a longing for the brightness and joy of Easter. Likewise, some churches will abstain from using the word 'Alleluia' or any of its cognates, so that when the congregation acclaim, 'He is risen indeed, Alleluia', on Easter morning, they might feel a real and vivid contrast with the preceding season.

As we prepare for our forty days together in the wilderness, walking through the book of Numbers, let us pray that God will give us the grace to rely ever more fully on him.

For reflection

- In what ways can we make our whole life a life of preparation?
- Do external means, such as the practice of Lent in general or the rituals of Ash Wednesday, help or hinder our preparation?

Prayer

Heavenly Father, as we prepare to enter the wilderness of Lent,
we know that we do not have it in us to make it to the promised land;
supply us with your grace, that we may be equipped to take hold of your promises,
through Jesus Christ our Lord.
Amen.

2
Fire

The Lord spoke to Moses and Aaron, saying: The Israelites shall camp
each in their respective regiments, under ensigns by their ancestral
houses; they shall camp facing the tent of meeting on every side . . .

    The tent of meeting, with the camp of the Levites, shall set out in
the centre of the camps; they shall set out just as they camp, each
in position, by their regiments.
(Numbers 2:1–2, 17)

And I heard a loud voice from the throne saying,

> 'See, the home of God is among mortals.
> He will dwell with them;
> they will be his peoples,
> and God himself will be with them;
> he will wipe every tear from their eyes.
> Death will be no more;
> mourning and crying and pain will be no more,
> for the first things have passed away.'

(Revelation 21:3–4)

When camping in the wild with a large group, there is a practice of
pitching tents in a circle around a central campfire. In this way, all the
campers can share the heat and light given off by the flames, as well as
sharing the responsibility of maintaining and managing the fire. Whether
for toasting marshmallows, or illuminating the way back to the tent, a
central fire can be a useful thing to cultivate. In a similar way, in the book
of Numbers, God is to be found literally in the middle of his people. Later
in the book, we will see God's presence marked by a pillar of cloud and
fire, which not only illuminates (and, we might presume, warms) his
people, but also guards and guides them.

Throughout the Bible, God makes known his desire to be in the centre of his people. Sometimes this centrality is literal and physical, such as in the wilderness journey and later in the Temple at Jerusalem. Here, we read how the tent of meeting, where God spoke to Moses, is placed in the middle of the tribes. The encamped people are to face towards the centre, where the presence of God is signified, much as we might think of tents around a campfire.

However, just as a campfire needs to be maintained and managed to mitigate the risk of it breaking out and burning up the campsite, the Israelite's experience of God teaches them something similar. The presence of God is not a thing to be trifled with, and the great mass of the people of God are to be kept at a distance from the tent of meeting and the holiness of the presence of God.

God's plan is still to be found in the midst of his people. The fullness of that will come, as the book of Revelation indicates, at the end of time; when God gathers all things to himself. If the fullness of God's plan is still far off, its beginnings are already well underway.

When John wrote the Gospel that bears his name, he was very careful about the words he chose. The phrase from John 1:14 that we may know as 'the Word became flesh and lived among us' might well be translated 'the Word became flesh and *pitched his tent* among us'. The allusion is to the tent of meeting from the book of Numbers. Jesus is God in the midst of his people.

As we continue to prepare to make this Lenten journey through the wilderness, we can take heart that we do not have a God who is far removed from us, and ring-fenced by priests whose job it is to keep us safely away. Rather, we have a God who has come very close to us, in the person of Jesus, our great high priest, who draws us safely into God's presence. Jesus will lead us into life with God – not by a pillar of cloud and fire, but by his word and Spirit.

For reflection

- When are you most aware of the presence of God?
- How can we be certain that God is in our midst, even when we don't feel it?

Prayer

Heavenly Father,
as we start out on this wilderness journey,
help us to keep you at the centre of our lives,
that we might always follow where you lead,
through Jesus Christ our Lord.
Amen.

3

Substitution

Then the LORD said to Moses: Enrol all the firstborn males of the Israelites, from a month old and upwards, and count their names. But you shall accept the Levites for me—I am the LORD—as substitutes for all the firstborn among the Israelites, and the livestock of the Levites as substitutes for all the firstborn among the livestock of the Israelites. So Moses enrolled all the firstborn among the Israelites, as the LORD commanded him. The total enrolment, all the firstborn males from a month old and upwards, counting the number of names, was twenty-two thousand two hundred and seventy-three.
(Numbers 3:40–3)

He is the image of the invisible God, the firstborn of all creation; for in him all things in heaven and on earth were created, things visible and invisible, whether thrones or dominions or rulers or powers— all things have been created through him and for him. He himself is before all things, and in him all things hold together. He is the head of the body, the church; he is the beginning, the firstborn from the dead, so that he might come to have first place in everything. For in him all the fullness of God was pleased to dwell, and through him God was pleased to reconcile to himself all things, whether on earth or in heaven, by making peace through the blood of his cross.
(Colossians 1:15–20)

Like many people, I began trying to avoid going into supermarkets during the Covid lockdowns of 2020. Since then, I have not felt any great desire to return to the aisles. Instead, I have taken to doing much of my grocery shopping online. When the delivery comes, the first thing I do is to check for substitutions, what has been swapped for what. Usually, the exchange is of little or no significance. Occasionally, the swap will seem a little bizarre – like getting tinned peaches instead of fresh fruit. But sometimes, if like me you are a person who almost always buys own-brand goods, they will send you an expensive brand rather than the cheaper item you had paid for. With joy in short supply during lockdown, this became one of life's little pleasures.

The theme of *substitution* runs throughout the book of Numbers. Indeed, substitution runs through the whole of the Bible, and spotting it when it crops up can help us to understand more clearly what God wants us to learn from these stories. As we begin to look at today's passage, we come to it knowing that the time that the people of God are to spend in the wilderness is to be a time of dedication.

In a similar way, our Lenten observances are a time of special dedication. This fits with our understanding of Sabbath. Although the whole of life was to be dedicated to God, yet in a strange way each Sabbath day was to be a day of complete dedication too. One short day as a particular substitute for the general devotion owed through the whole week. One part substituting or representing the whole.

There were also other ways in which the general dedication of God's people was to be represented by a substitution. One such sign of the general dedication which was expected of every Israelite was to be the particular offering of all firstborn sons, which we can also understand in the light of the Passover.

In that story, which we read about in Exodus, God has brought the people out from slavery in Egypt. As we read, we learn how Pharaoh has stubbornly refused to release God's people from their bonds of slavery. Despite wavering occasionally, he will not release the Israelites even in the face of increasingly severe plagues. Each plague carries symbolic value. In the first plague, which is the turning of water into blood, we see a foreshadowing of the death that is on the horizon. That death comes in the climax of these plagues: the death of the firstborn. The Israelites are exempted from this final plague, not because of their innocence but because of the mercy of God.

As the people were redeemed in general, so the Israelite firstborn were redeemed in particular. As the people were to be dedicated to God in general, so the firstborn were to be dedicated in particular. It is the particularity of this redemption of the firstborn sons that is addressed in our passage from Numbers. Understanding substitution here is essential if we hope to understand substitution each time it appears in Numbers and the whole of the Bible. Here we see that each one of the firstborn sons is spared from exclusive lifelong service to God by a Levite representative who will take his place in service at the sanctuary.

This itself is a picture. It illustrates the great value that God the Father places on God the Son. God the Son is made known to us in the person of Jesus Christ. Jesus is the only Son of God, and upon the cross he takes our place by offering his own life in total dedication to the Father. As we dedicate this period of time, our wilderness journey, we do so following the pattern of devotion and dedicated service that Jesus lived out; but, more than this, we do so knowing that he has redeemed us by taking our place.

For reflection

- How did Jesus live out his dedication to God?
- What can we do to dedicate our lives more fully to God?

Prayer

Heavenly Father, as this season of Lent stretches before us,
give us grace to remain devoted to you,
so that we can grow in holiness and likeness to your Son,
and praise him for all that he has done.
Amen.

4

Body

The service of the Kohathites relating to the tent of meeting concerns the most holy things.

When the camp is to set out, Aaron and his sons shall go in and take down the screening curtain, and cover the ark of the covenant with it; then they shall put on it a covering of fine leather, and spread over that a cloth all of blue, and shall put its poles in place . . .

When Aaron and his sons have finished covering the sanctuary and all the furnishings of the sanctuary, as the camp sets out, after that the Kohathites shall come to carry these, but they must not touch the holy things, or they will die. These are the things of the tent of meeting that the Kohathites are to carry.
(Numbers 4:4–6, 15)

For by the grace given to me I say to everyone among you not to think of yourself more highly than you ought to think, but to think with sober judgement, each according to the measure of faith that God has assigned. For as in one body we have many members, and not all the members have the same function, so we, who are many, are one body in Christ, and individually we are members one of another.
(Romans 12:3–5)

When I was at university I sang in a choir. It might be quite generous of me to describe what I did as *singing*. I certainly tried to sing, but I didn't always achieve my aim. After a few of weeks of attending, following along with the various bits of music and finding my place, finally I was apportioned a lot with the basses. There were a couple of good reasons why the choirmaster gave me the bass line to sing. First, I was encouraged to understand that there were few other men on the bass line and they needed the support. Second, it was made clear to me that being a bass meant that

I didn't have to worry about trying to sing any of the difficult parts that would be expected of the tenors and baritones.

This was not so much about where I best fitted in. Rather, it was about finding the best place to keep me until I learned how to sing more reliably.

It is not so in the wilderness journey of God's people. There, on the edge of existence, everyone has a part to play. No one is just *kept busy* or out of the way. Whether it is to bear the sword, to offer sacrifices or to carry the special items which make up God's palace-tent, his dwelling place among his people, no one is a passenger. Everyone has a task.

In our Christian life, we often use the analogy of a body. The Bible teaches us that the Church is the body of Christ. This is a body which has many parts, all of which need to work together. Sometimes, it can be easy to know what part we must play; for example, the clergy. At other times, someone will helpfully point us in the right direction, as my choirmaster did for me. However, we will often need to do some of this figuring-out for ourselves. God is not going to give us specific instructions as he does for the Kohathites in our reading, but he has already given us general instructions in his word.

We know what God wants: whether it is to feed the hungry, clothe the naked, tend the sick or visit the prisoner, God wants us to do good works and to give him the glory. We also know that, as Christians, none of our good works can happen successfully without the proclamation of the gospel and the undergirding of prayer. We know what needs to be done, and so each must discern how to use our gifts, abilities and talents to best serve the needs of the Church and the world.

When my children were very young, they would play with variously shaped blocks, which would fit snugly in the appropriate gap. There is a saying, isn't there? 'Being a square peg in a round hole' means being the wrong person for the job. As Christians, we must find the right work of service and then we must give ourselves fully to that task.

The Kohathites are able to fulfil their God-given vocation most fully when they get stuck into the work that has been given to them. Thinking back to our bodily metaphor, feet are most fully feet when we walk on them, eyes are most fully eyes when we see with them, and so we will most fully fulfil our vocation and calling as members of the one body when we give ourselves most fully to that task and do it.

For reflection

- What part are you to play in the body of Christ?
- How has God equipped you to fulfil that calling?

Prayer

Almighty God, help me to sing the song which you have given me;
train me to play the part which you have prepared;
use me in the way that you would;
so that I can join with all your people,
in service and praise.
Amen.

Part 1

REVELATION AT SINAI
B. Preparing to take the land
(Numbers 5:1 – 10:10)

As the Israelites ready themselves to follow God's command to take hold of the promised land, and with it secure all the promises of God to their forefather Abraham, the people receive new sets of laws and regulations. These rules make sense in the context of a people who are learning what it means to live together as a nation of free people. Liberated from the yoke of slavery, they are to govern their own behaviour according to a distinctive pattern of life. This is a way of living that tells us something about the God whom they serve and the relationship that exists between God and his people – and by extension God and us as his people in this age.

The first week in Lent

Monday: unclean (Numbers 5:1–4)
Tuesday: adultery (Numbers 5:11–15)
Wednesday: nazirite (Numbers 6:1–4)
Thursday: peace (Numbers 6:22–7)
Friday: speak (Numbers 7:89 – 8:3)
Saturday: Passover (Numbers 9:9–14)

5

Unclean

The LORD spoke to Moses, saying: Command the Israelites to put out of the camp everyone who is leprous, or has a discharge, and everyone who is unclean through contact with a corpse; you shall put out both male and female, putting them outside the camp; they must not defile their camp, where I dwell among them. The Israelites did so, putting them outside the camp; as the LORD had spoken to Moses, so the Israelites did.
(Numbers 5:1–4)

A leper came to him begging him, and kneeling he said to him, 'If you choose, you can make me clean.' Moved with pity, Jesus stretched out his hand and touched him, and said to him, 'I do choose. Be made clean!' Immediately the leprosy left him, and he was made clean. After sternly warning him he sent him away at once, saying to him, 'See that you say nothing to anyone; but go, show yourself to the priest, and offer for your cleansing what Moses commanded, as a testimony to them.' But he went out and began to proclaim it freely, and to spread the word, so that Jesus could no longer go into a town openly, but stayed out in the country; and people came to him from every quarter.
(Mark 1:40–5)

During the summer break while I was at university, I worked in a petrol station. It was a medium-sized service station, just off the M5. Not only did we sell fuel, but we also stocked a range of pasties and snack products, all at an obscene price. In the short induction course that all the staff had to attend prior to their first shift, we were taught that, whereas in other customer-service roles 'the customer comes first', when it comes to selling fuel 'safety comes first'. Mercifully, incidents at petrol stations are rare, because of the rigorous rules and regulations that govern how they operate.

Life in the ancient camp of the Lord is to be no different. Rules and regulations designed, in part, to keep the people safe dominate this part of the story of God's people. Here, we see that the safety of the whole nation is always to trump the well-being of the individual. It might be a ruinous thing for a man or woman to be put outside the camp, but better that than have the whole community succumb to infection. This would mean not only greater loss of life, but also the loss of the promises of God which are being worked out in their midst.

Safety is to come first, and this meant putting purity first. Not only do purity regulations help to prevent cross-contamination and widespread, fast-moving plagues of sickness, but they also serve to highlight something about the distinction between the people and their God.

The people are frail and prone to diseases. The diseases which the people transmit to one another serve as an illustration of the way in which they are prone to transmitting false and destructive ideas about themselves, God, and how the relationship between them was to be managed. God, on the other hand, is not subject to change. He is not frail, nor is he prone to disease of any kind, physical or spiritual. His purity, his *holiness*, is unchanging from eternity to eternity.

Jesus, when confronted with impurity, far from shrinking back (as though he might *catch* something) presses in closer. Jesus touches lepers and makes them clean in order to teach us that by his touch he can make us holy. In Jesus, the fear of transmission is reversed. Power, glory, love go out from him, changing everyone with whom he comes into contact. Jesus, by his Holy Spirit, can cleanse us from the leprosy of sin and restore us to new life.

The same Jesus who touches lepers and makes them clean wants his Church to continue this work of bringing wholeness, healing and purity today. We are to carry this love which makes us holy into all the areas of our lives where it will do good to those who encounter it. In my petrol station, safety was to come first; but in the Church, love is to come first. Because it is the love of God in Jesus Christ that is able to make us eternally safe.

For reflection

- What personal sins do you need Jesus to cleanse?
- How can we be certain that Jesus will cleanse us from all our sin? See 1 John 1:9.

23

Prayer

Jesus, we thank you that you reached out your hand to cleanse from disease;

reach out your hand now and cleanse my heart from the disease of sin.

Come to me, and share your holiness with me, welcoming me into your presence.

Amen.

6
Adultery

The LORD spoke to Moses, saying: Speak to the Israelites and say to them: If any man's wife goes astray and is unfaithful to him, if a man has had intercourse with her but it is hidden from her husband, so that she is undetected though she has defiled herself, and there is no witness against her since she was not caught in the act; if a spirit of jealousy comes on him, and he is jealous of his wife who has defiled herself; or if a spirit of jealousy comes on him, and he is jealous of his wife, though she has not defiled herself; then the man shall bring his wife to the priest. And he shall bring the offering required for her, one-tenth of an ephah of barley flour. He shall pour no oil on it and put no frankincense on it, for it is a grain-offering of jealousy, a grain-offering of remembrance, bringing iniquity to remembrance.
(Numbers 5:11–15)

The scribes and the Pharisees brought a woman who had been caught in adultery; and making her stand before all of them, they said to him, 'Teacher, this woman was caught in the very act of committing adultery ... Jesus straightened up and said to her, 'Woman, where are they? Has no one condemned you?' She said, 'No one, sir.' And Jesus said, 'Neither do I condemn you. Go your way, and from now on do not sin again.'
(John 8:3–4, 10–11)

The Wicked Bible of 1631, also called the Adulterous Bible or the Sinners' Bible, is a rare edition of the King James Bible which contains a serious error. In lieu of the seventh commandment, 'Thou shalt not commit adultery', the misprint reads, 'Thou shalt commit adultery.' As soon as the mistake was spotted, as many copies as could be gathered were destroyed, leaving only a few left today. Charles I, who was king at the time, and his

25

Archbishop of Canterbury were furious at the mistake. They had the publishers fined £300, more than £50,000 in today's money.

In the Bible, the contrasting themes of faithfulness and adultery are used literally, metaphorically and sometimes both at once, often intimating at different parts of Scripture such as the echo of Numbers 5 in John 8.[1] The Bible takes adultery very seriously, and so should we. It destroys families, breaks communities and leaves countless individual lives poorer, but this is not the deepest level at which the Bible is opposed to this sort of behaviour. God requires us to be faithful in our relationships because he is faithful. Insofar as we are faithful, we emulate his faithfulness to us and grow in our likeness to him. Infidelity makes us less like God, and further separates us from his presence.

Throughout the Bible, God likens the relationship he has with his people to a marriage. Again and again, God tells them that he loves them dearly, but that their idolatry (worshipping of idols or other gods) is a form of spiritual adultery. God's people time and again give the loyalty and affection that they had promised to their God to other things. We can see this acted out in the story of the exodus. There, the people of Israel gather at Mount Sinai, in the place where the story of the book of Numbers begins. There, God's people are given the Ten Commandments, as a covenant is enacted between God and his people. Promises and obligations are exchanged. In a sense, the Ten Commandments act much like a set of marriage vows. And yet, before the ink is dry, the people are worshipping a golden calf. God's people, like all people, are prone to spiritual adultery.

In the New Testament, we see this language change in a slight, but meaningful way. Linguistically, Jesus takes God's place as husband. Jesus being the same God but now incarnate. The message is the same, however: God in Christ is faithful. But the message of the Bible goes beyond this. God is more than just faithful, he is faithful to us even when we are not faithful to him. He loves us even when we do not love him but, by pouring his love into our hearts, he transforms us. He will make good on all his promises to bring us to his heavenly wedding banquet at the consummation of creation, when Jesus is wedded to his bride, the Church.

We are all prone to spiritual adultery, the desire to give our love and affection to things that do not deserve it, instead of to God. But God, in

---

1 For a fuller exploration of the way Old Testament themes echo in the New Testament, see N. Lunn, *The Gospels Through Old Testament Eyes: Exploring extended allusions* (London: Apollos, 2023).

Jesus, offers us forgiveness and restoration. Each time, he picks us up and speaks those words: 'Neither do I condemn you. Go your way, and from now on do not sin again.'

For reflection
- In what ways are you prone to be unfaithful to God?
- What sorts of behaviour show a heart that is faithful to God?

Prayer
Father, we thank you that you are a faithful God,
and that Jesus is faithful to his Church.
Send your Holy Spirit into our hearts,
so that we can be presented holy and faithful on the last day.
Amen.

7

Nazirite

The LORD spoke to Moses, saying: Speak to the Israelites and say to them: When either men or women make a special vow, the vow of a nazirite, to separate themselves to the LORD, they shall separate themselves from wine and strong drink; they shall drink no wine vinegar or other vinegar, and shall not drink any grape juice or eat grapes, fresh or dried. All their days as nazirites they shall eat nothing that is produced by the grape-vine, not even the seeds or the skins.

(Numbers 6:1–4)

I appeal to you therefore, brothers and sisters, by the mercies of God, to present your bodies as a living sacrifice, holy and acceptable to God, which is your spiritual worship. Do not be conformed to this world, but be transformed by the renewing of your minds, so that you may discern what is the will of God—what is good and acceptable and perfect.

(Romans 12:1–2)

The ancient people of Israel were arranged in a *hierarchy.* The nation was divided into ranks of holiness, or concentric circles of sanctity. The largest circle encompassed all the people of Israel: by their circumcision and keeping of Sabbath, they were set apart as a holy nation. Within this mass of people, the tribe of the Levites were also set apart. The Levites were deprived of territorial inheritance, so their inheritance was to be God himself. This was worked out in the Levites' service around the tent of meeting, where God met with Moses. Within the tribe of Levites, there was a further distinction, a particular caste of priests, descendants of Aaron's family. Their role was to offer sacrifices.

The system was rigid, but there was a built-in way of circumnavigating the arranged ranks in order to get closer to God. This was to make a special vow, the vow of the nazirite. By taking this vow, any person from the nation was able to dedicate themselves to God by setting themselves apart. Often in our day-to-day life, we like to mark things out as special. My mother used to keep a *special* set of crockery for when we were receiving guests, and for Christmas or other occasions. There actually wasn't anything particularly special about these plates, but they felt special because of the way that they were treated and how they were used. We have an incredible ability as people to sort almost anything, seemingly arbitrarily, into two different piles: sacred and profane. Special and ordinary. We do it with the foods we eat, for example saving cake for birthdays, or pastries for breakfast at the weekend.

The nazirites were marked out by their avoidance of wine or anything to do with grapes. This gave them special privileges, comparable to those of the priesthood, as people who were holy to God. John the Baptist was one such nazirite, consecrated from before his birth.

Now that Jesus has come and redeemed us by his blood, this old hierarchy has been fulfilled and is no longer binding on Christians. By joining ourselves to Christ, we participate in his high priesthood, as 'a priestly kingdom and a holy nation' (Exodus 19:6). Although there is now no longer a hierarchy to circumvent, nevertheless each one of us is called to a life of holiness that is pleasing to God. Unlike the nazirites, we do not need to abstain from alcohol – although we may do so if we believe it will help us to live holy lives. What is more important is that we seek to find out what patterns of behaviour are most pleasing to God, and conform our own lives to that.

This is only possible in the power of the Spirit, who gives more than just the strength to live a transformed life. The Holy Spirit renews our hearts and our minds so that we desire the good things of God.

For reflection

- Ancient Israel was hierarchical – is the Church supposed to be hierarchical too?
- Should Christians take special vows?

Prayer

Father, you have called us to be a priestly kingdom,
give us the grace of your Holy Spirit
so that we can share in the priesthood of Christ,

and so offer the whole of our lives in sacrifice to you;
that your name might be worshipped throughout the world,
Amen.

8
Peace

The LORD spoke to Moses, saying: Speak to Aaron and his sons, saying, Thus you shall bless the Israelites: you shall say to them,

> The LORD bless you and keep you;
> the LORD make his face to shine upon you, and be gracious
> to you;
> the LORD lift up his countenance upon you, and give you peace.

So they shall put my name on the Israelites, and I will bless them.
(Numbers 6:22–7)

Do not worry about anything, but in everything by prayer and supplication with thanksgiving let your requests be made known to God. And the peace of God, which surpasses all understanding, will guard your hearts and your minds in Christ Jesus . . .
Keep on doing the things that you have learned and received and heard and seen in me, and the God of peace will be with you.
(Philippians 4:6–7, 9)

God desires peace for his people. The peace that God wants us to know and experience is not simply the absence of conflict or strife. Rather, the peace that God wants for us is a *wholeness* that is secured by the abiding presence of God himself. This presence is made manifest in the bearing of his name. God wants this peace-in-presence for us, and he offers it to us. Throughout the book of Numbers, the Israelites are learning to live with the presence of God in their midst. There are visible signs of the presence of God throughout this wilderness journey. Such signs are the pillar of fire and cloud that hovers over the tabernacle before departing to lead the people out; and the presence of God above the mercy seat, that spot on top of the ark of the covenant where the Ten Commandments were kept, which would later reside in the Holy of Holies in the Temple at Jerusalem.

These visible signs are not lasting. The pillar of fire and cloud disperses after its purpose has been fulfilled; and the glory of God is seen in prophecy departing from the Temple. But this grand and visible presence is only one aspect of the fullness of the presence of God. There is another aspect: the Israelites' bearing of God's name.

The presence of God is personal and intimate for those who put their trust in him, and who take his name upon themselves. In the Aaronic blessing of peace, the prayer of blessing or benediction builds up to a great crescendo. The prayer invokes the shining of God's face upon his people, and the lifting up of his countenance, as preludes to this gift of peace. Here we discover the means by which the loving presence of God is to be proclaimed to his people as an agent of inner peace: God's name.

As the Israelites make their way through the wilderness and draw near to the promised land, they are to know the peace that comes from God's presence – and God's presence is manifest in his name. It is as though they will not be able to discern God's peace in the promised land, if they do not first learn how to bear his name here in the wilderness. The promised land itself prefigures the peace of God, which arrives in its fullness in the life that is after this one, when God's people are gathered into the heavenly Jerusalem.

To know this peace is to rest in God, in joy and in sorrow; in good times and in bad. It is a peace which, if cultivated, can carry us through any wilderness period that we encounter on our journey of faith. The God whose peace is proclaimed by Aaron and his priestly descendants is the same God who has made himself known in Jesus Christ. When Jesus is born, the angelic choir sing of peace on earth because Jesus comes to make this peace available to everyone who turns to God in faith. Whereas, in former times, this peace was reserved for one nation, now all those who come to Christ take upon themselves the triune name in baptism and, following his ways, can know this peace, which is given by the abiding presence of the Holy Spirit.

For reflection

- What does it feel like to know the peace of God?
- Is this feeling something you can cultivate or work at – or is it just a gift?

Prayer

Father, we thank you for the peace which you have won for us;
through the death of your Son you have ended the enmity between us;
now through your Spirit work your peace into every aspect of our lives.
Amen.

9

Speak

When Moses went into the tent of meeting to speak with the LORD, he would hear the voice speaking to him from above the mercy-seat that was on the ark of the covenant from between the two cherubim; thus it spoke to him.

The LORD spoke to Moses, saying: Speak to Aaron and say to him: When you set up the lamps, the seven lamps shall give light in front of the lampstand. Aaron did so; he set up its lamps to give light in front of the lampstand, as the LORD had commanded Moses.
(Numbers 7:89 – 8:3)

Then I turned to see whose voice it was that spoke to me, and on turning I saw seven golden lampstands, and in the midst of the lampstands I saw one like the Son of Man, clothed with a long robe and with a golden sash across his chest.
(Revelation 1:12–13)

God is a verbal God;[1] he is a God who speaks. The voice of God is creative, it calls existence into being. In Genesis, we are told that God said, 'Let there be light', and there was light. Later in the same book come the first words of God to humanity. There, God hands over something of his creativity by his words to Adam and Eve, as he says, 'Be fruitful and multiply.' Influenced by these ideas, John's Gospel displays a similar mix of word, light and creation. There, John says that Jesus is the Word of God, and the light of the world, by whom all things were made. God's words are tied to both light and creation.

In Numbers, God speaks to his prophet, Moses. Numbers is, on the face of it, an account of God giving directions so that God's people can come to know how they are to relate to their Creator, the conditions under which

---

1 R. Holland, 'Expository Preaching: The Robust Response to a Logical Bibliology', *The Master's Seminary Journal* 22.1 (2011), 19–39.

God will reside with them, and how he will continue to speak to them. The voice of God will give light and material blessing.

Since the beginning, God has not stopped speaking to his people. The Bible is both the record of God's voice and the means by which he speaks. God breathed life into the work of the human authors so that he is revealed by what we read there. In this sense, the Bible is the word of God. Psalm 119 calls God's word a light and a lamp. It illuminates our path. It is the light by which we not only see what is in front of us, but are also helped to understand the source of light itself.

The lampstand that stood in the tabernacle in our reading from the book of Numbers was built and positioned to shine its light forward to fall upon the twelve loaves of the presence, which symbolised God's material blessing of the twelve tribes of Israel.

God continues to bless his people; and the material blessings which he spreads across all people in all places are supplemented by the spiritual blessings which are for those who know him by faith. Jesus walks in the midst of the golden lampstands. In every place where Jesus is proclaimed from the lamp of God's word, Jesus blesses us with his presence, as he makes his home within us by his Holy Spirit.

For reflection

- How does God's word act as a lamp for your path?
- What can we do if we want to see the way ahead more clearly?

Prayer

Father, your word is light and life;
speak into our hearts
so that we may be enlightened by your truth,
made anew in your love,
and come to know the blessing of your abiding presence with us:
through the mediation of Jesus Christ our Lord.
Amen.

10

Passover

The LORD spoke to Moses, saying: Speak to the Israelites, saying: Anyone of you or your descendants who is unclean through touching a corpse, or is away on a journey, shall still keep the passover to the LORD. In the second month on the fourteenth day, at twilight, they shall keep it; they shall eat it with unleavened bread and bitter herbs. They shall leave none of it until morning, nor break a bone of it; according to all the statute for the passover they shall keep it. But anyone who is clean and is not on a journey, and yet refrains from keeping the passover, shall be cut off from the people for not presenting the LORD's offering at its appointed time; such a one shall bear the consequences for the sin. Any alien residing among you who wishes to keep the passover to the Lord shall do so according to the statute of the passover and according to its regulation; you shall have one statute for both the resident alien and the native.
(Numbers 9:9–14)

After this, Jesus went to the other side of the Sea of Galilee, also called the Sea of Tiberias. A large crowd kept following him, because they saw the signs that he was doing for the sick. Jesus went up the mountain and sat down there with his disciples. Now the Passover, the festival of the Jews, was near. When he looked up and saw a large crowd coming towards him, Jesus said to Philip, 'Where are we to buy bread for these people to eat?'
(John 6:1–5)

A good friend of mine from Bible college is married to an American woman. I used to live upstairs from them in my maisonette. They would be sure always to invite me to the various American-style events that they would host on US holidays. At Thanksgiving there would be a fantastic spread, but the greatest party was, of course, 4 July. For Americans, this day recalls not only a great day of joy, but also liberation. America doesn't have an established religion, but I might suggest that 4 July comes pretty close.

I am not sure there is anything that really resonates with 4 July in the UK; you might disagree. However, I do think there is a similarity between 4 July and the Jewish Passover. At the Passover, faithful Jews eat and drink in remembrance and celebration of their liberation from slavery in Egypt. At the first Passover, each family sacrificed a lamb, covered their lintel with its blood, and ate the lamb roasted along with unleavened bread. God liberates; God provides.

This is the context into which Jesus is speaking as we read his words at the beginning of the story of the Feeding of the Five Thousand in John's Gospel. John tells us that the Passover is at hand, and Jesus is using this as an occasion to illustrate his teaching. All through the Gospel, Jesus has been teaching – both out in the open and in the synagogue. As the story moves on to the feeding of this great multitude and then beyond, we see the audience gathered around Jesus dwindle from a large crowd, perhaps as many as thirty thousand people, down eventually to just the disciples by the end of chapter 6.

Jesus has been teaching that he is a new and greater Moses, who has come to lead the people on a new and greater exodus.

In fact, Jesus teaches that all the stories of God's mighty acts of liberation and provision in the Old Testament find new and fuller meaning in him. Not only is Jesus proposing to lead his people in an exodus from the slavery of sin to the liberty of faith – but he also teaches that he himself will be the provision along the way. His blood is the blood that makes us safe, and his flesh given for the life of the world is the food that sustains us. He is the one that sustains, not just through the years of wilderness wandering, but all the way into eternal life.

For reflection

- From what things in your life has Jesus led you in an exodus?
- How does Jesus provide himself as sustenance along the way?

Prayer

Father, we thank you for the joy you have brought us in Jesus Christ;
help us to take hold of the liberation that he offers through his cross,
so that in freedom from sin we can feast on the true food that is his life,
and drink deeply of the water that is his Spirit.
Amen.

Part 2

FROM SINAI TO KADESH (NUMBERS 10:11 – 12:16)

God's people are on the move as they begin their journey through the wilderness and yet, despite God being in their midst, sin encroaches. We see dissent and rebellion against God and against his plan of salvation. The wilderness has much to teach the people, but they are not yet ready to learn all the lessons that come their way.

The second week in Lent

Monday: move (Numbers 10:11–16)
Tuesday: family (Numbers 10:29–32)
Wednesday: scatter (Numbers 10:33–6)
Thursday: meat (Numbers 11:4–6)
Friday: spirit (Numbers 11:24–9)
Saturday: humble (Numbers 12:1–8)

11

Move

In the second year, in the second month, on the twentieth day of the month, the cloud lifted from over the tabernacle of the covenant. Then the Israelites set out by stages from the wilderness of Sinai, and the cloud settled down in the wilderness of Paran. They set out for the first time at the command of the LORD by Moses. The standard of the camp of Judah set out first, company by company, and over the whole company was Nahshon son of Amminadab. Over the company of the tribe of Issachar was Nethanel son of Zuar; and over the company of the tribe of Zebulun was Eliab son of Helon. (Numbers 10:11–16)

Now the eleven disciples went to Galilee, to the mountain to which Jesus had directed them. When they saw him, they worshipped him; but some doubted. And Jesus came and said to them, 'All authority in heaven and on earth has been given to me. Go therefore and make disciples of all nations, baptizing them in the name of the Father and of the Son and of the Holy Spirit, and teaching them to obey everything that I have commanded you. And remember, I am with you always, to the end of the age.'
(Matthew 28:16–20)

One of the things about being a young member of the clergy that really does take quite some getting used to is all the moving you must do. In the space of a few short years, I moved from my home to Bible college, and from there to my first curacy, before moving again to my second curacy, all within about six years – who knows when I may need to move again? I know that this is the same for people in a range of different careers. My brother is in the Armed Forces; I know that he has had a similar experience. Although there isn't a lifting of the cloud, as in our reading from Numbers, the great thing about relocating as a follower of Jesus (whether we are clergy, soldiers or anyone prayerfully considering the next step of their life) is the sense that we move because we are sent by God.

God is a God who sends. So much that we read in the Bible has to do with God sending. Indeed, we can think of the Gospel itself as a series of 'sendings'. First, humanity is sent away from the garden of Eden at the Fall; this is humanity's first experience of being called to move, but the story doesn't end there. In the fullness of time, God sends his Son to bring us back. Having returned to his Father, the Son now sends his Spirit into our hearts; and this Spirit sends us to the ends of the world to proclaim all that God has done for us. The Gospel is a story where God moves and calls us to move with him.

As we read the Bible, we discover that God often calls upon his people to move, as he sends them from one place to another. This physical movement almost always corresponds to a spiritual meaning which is greater or more significant than the move itself. We might think of the call of Abraham, and his sending to the promised land, which corresponds to Abraham's spiritual movement from idolatry to the worship of the one true God. We might think also of the call of the patriarchs into Egypt by the summons of Joseph, which teaches us about God's providence and provision. As we get to the New Testament, we see Jesus telling his disciples to move from town to town, as he empowers them to proclaim the gospel in word and deed, and powerful signs. Finally, in our snippet from the Gospel of Matthew we see the commissioning of the disciples – and in it the promised movement of the good news from Jerusalem out into all nations.

As Christians, we are called by God to move outwards with the gospel. For some people, this is a call to traditional missionary work, to take the message about Jesus to foreign countries. For many of us, however, the call is to move to a new spiritual location – as we proclaim Jesus in our friendship groups, in our workplaces and in our home towns. As we move, the Church moves with us.

We can go as far as to say that God is always on the move in Scripture. Although, strictly speaking, God is always everywhere, his manifest presence and power can be said to be on the move as he goes before us, comes alongside us and follows us, as we move out proclaiming his word.

He is with us, and promises to remain with us, as we move. It is fair to say that the Church is undergoing a great deal of movement in our age, as it seeks to respond to, and minister within, a rapidly changing culture – but this has always been true, because God is a God who moves, and who calls us to move. Let us trust God and follow him as we move forward.

For reflection

- Has God ever asked you to move, either on your own or with your family?
- Have you ever felt God moving you spiritually, perhaps from one opinion to another?

Prayer

We pray, Lord Jesus, that you will always be one step ahead of us on the road, preparing the way.

We pray that you will be beside us on the journey, guiding our steps.

We pray that you will be at the end of all our travels to welcome us home. Amen.

12
Family

Moses said to Hobab son of Reuel the Midianite, Moses' father-in-law, 'We are setting out for the place of which the LORD said, "I will give it to you"; come with us, and we will treat you well; for the LORD has promised good to Israel.' But he said to him, 'I will not go, but I will go back to my own land and to my kindred.' He said, 'Do not leave us, for you know where we should camp in the wilderness, and you will serve as eyes for us. Moreover, if you go with us, whatever good the LORD does for us, the same we will do for you.'
(Numbers 10:29–32)

Then his mother and his brothers came; and standing outside, they sent to him and called him. A crowd was sitting around him; and they said to him, 'Your mother and your brothers and sisters are outside, asking for you.' And he replied, 'Who are my mother and my brothers?' And looking at those who sat around him, he said, 'Here are my mother and my brothers! Whoever does the will of God is my brother and sister and mother.'
(Mark 3:31–5)

As God's people begin to move forward through the wilderness and as we journey through Numbers, we can begin to reflect on the way in which God intends us to move forward as Christians in the twenty-first century. What can we learn from the way in which Israel set out, and how can we apply what we learn to our own journeys through the modern wilderness? Importantly, from this passage we see that we are not to try to go alone.

Numbers presents God's salvation as worked out through an extended human family. This is made clear in the way in which God's people are to arrange their camp, and the way in which they set out, together, in family groups. This is the repeated message through the Old Testament. We see again and again the universal hope of God's blessing promised and secured through the particular blessing of one family: the children of Abraham, Israel. In our reading today, Hobab is faced with a choice between remaining with his natural family, his kinsfolk, or joining the family of Abraham.

Although there are vital roles for individuals in the story of God and his people, these individuals exist and function as particular parts within the larger body. These separate parts frequently rely on those around them for practical support.

In a similar way, it is impossible to be a Lone Ranger Christian. Instead, we are to be part of God's family, the Church. The grace of the Holy Spirit that makes Christians into a new family in Christ does not abolish the old natural order of family units; but it perfects it, offering a context for each family unit to exist together in greater harmony, without division based on ethnicity or national heritage. The Church, as God's people, fulfils the promise to Abraham that, through him, all nations will be blessed; because the Church is the family into which all families may come, no matter their shape or size. Unlike Hobab, we do not need to leave our kinsfolk physically in order to be part of God's family.

In Numbers, God's people are arranged by family so that every person has a place where they belong and a group of people with whom they can build a mutual interdependence, relying on each other through the hardships of life. As many of us will know from our own lives, and as we discover from the fractures and failures in family life, the natural family cannot be the answer to every problem that we encounter in our wilderness journey – indeed, our natural family may be a source of pain or frustration. As we set out on God's mission, to proclaim the good news about Jesus to a world which is under judgement, we find ourselves similarly arranged. For better or worse, all of us have a natural family, and many of us will have the experience of marrying into a new family, but as Christians we find ourselves welcomed and adopted into God's family. This new family finds one expression in our local church where we are able to build relationships of mutual interdependence – helping others, as they help us through the hardships of our modern wilderness.

For reflection

- Did your family life help or hinder your growth as a Christian?
- Have you found the Church to be like a family?

Prayer

Father, from whom every family derives its name, I pray that out of your glorious riches you will strengthen us with power through your Spirit, that Christ may dwell in our hearts through faith; so that we, being rooted and established in him, may have power, together with all the Lord's holy family, to grasp how wide and long and high and deep is the love of Christ; to you be glory in the Church and in Christ Jesus throughout all generations, for ever and ever! Amen.

(Ephesians 3.14–21, adapted)

13
Scatter

So they set out from the mount of the Lord on three days' journey with the ark of the covenant of the Lord going before them three days' journey, to seek out a resting-place for them, the cloud of the Lord being over them by day when they set out from the camp. Whenever the ark set out, Moses would say,

'Arise, O Lord, let your enemies be scattered,
  and your foes flee before you.'

And whenever it came to rest, he would say,

'Return, O Lord of the ten thousand thousands of Israel.'
(Numbers 10:33–6)

Finally, be strong in the Lord and in the strength of his power. Put on the whole armour of God, so that you may be able to stand against the wiles of the devil. For our struggle is not against enemies of blood and flesh, but against the rulers, against the authorities, against the cosmic powers of this present darkness, against the spiritual forces of evil in the heavenly places. Therefore take up the whole armour of God, so that you may be able to withstand on that evil day, and having done everything, to stand firm.
(Ephesians 6:10–13)

The 2002 fantasy film *The Lord of the Rings: The Two Towers* does a fantastic job of depicting J. R. R. Tolkien's book of the same name. There is a particular scene where many of the heroes are besieged, seemingly without hope, in the mountainside fortress of Helm's Deep. But then, seemingly out of nowhere, the enemies are scattered. The assembled ranks of orcs (Tolkien's metaphor for the forces of evil and destruction) are engaged, and overrun, by a last-minute cavalry charge down a steep embankment. This battle-changing charge is led by the wizard, Gandalf the White. Gandalf is a fascinating character throughout Tolkien's deeply Catholic work. Popping up time and again, older than the world itself, and often acting in a way that is understandable only to himself, Gandalf is an enigma. Although his character is not analogous to Jesus in a straightforward way (as is Aslan, for example, in C. S. Lewis's Chronicles of Narnia), nevertheless Tolkien uses the character of Gandalf to portray some Christ-like themes throughout the story.

Can we think of this cavalry charge as being in any way Christ-like?

In our reading from Numbers, we hear the plea go up from Moses asking God to scatter his enemies. We might have some well-founded reticence about using this sort of language. Despite our concerns, we cannot escape the reality – the Bible frequently talks in these terms. Accordingly, we must not rush to write off this language as merely the nationalistic rhetoric of a Bronze Age people. Although it is true that many people of many religions have envisaged a war-like or militaristic deity being on their side in conflict, nevertheless, when we take the Bible seriously on its own terms, we are able to see much more in this and similar texts.

God is, indeed, a God who scatters his enemies; and we must learn to understand the importance and utility of such language here in the book of Numbers, if we hope to understand the person and work of Christ in the New Testament. Therefore, in the Old Testament, we see the story of God's victory over temporal or earthly enemies, as a sign or type of the ultimate victory that he will win over the spiritual enemies of evil, sin and death.

In Numbers, God scatters the earthly enemies of his people, as a token of the scattering of evil that will in time take place. If we can conceive of 'the rulers, authorities and cosmic powers of this present darkness' as well as 'the spiritual forces of evil in the heavenly places' (cf. Ephesians 6.10–13) as being our enemies in a way no less real or true than the enemies scattered by God in the book of Numbers, we will learn to trust in the all-conquering might of the God who scatters his enemies. Although we cannot see these spiritual realities, they are our true enemies. They are the things that do harm to God's people and wage war against his kingdom; but rooted in our reading of Numbers, we can be assured that God will do harm to the things that do us harm. This he achieves in the death of Jesus Christ, where our greatest enemy, death itself, is put to death.

When Christ returns, all evil will be scattered before him, as he calls us home to rest.

For reflection

- What evil in your life do you need God to scatter?
- How does he do the work of scattering his enemies in this life?

Prayer

Father God,
scatter the arranged powers of darkness that beset us in this world,
and spread your light in our life by the presence of your Spirit.
Amen.

14
Meat

The rabble among them had a strong craving; and the Israelites also wept again, and said, 'If only we had meat to eat! We remember the fish we used to eat in Egypt for nothing, the cucumbers, the melons, the leeks, the onions, and the garlic; but now our strength is dried up, and there is nothing at all but this manna to look at.'
(Numbers 11:4–6)

Those who eat my flesh and drink my blood have eternal life, and I will raise them up on the last day; for my flesh is true food and my blood is true drink. Those who eat my flesh and drink my blood abide in me, and I in them.
(John 6:54–6)

We pick up with God's people today, on their journey through the wilderness, as they begin to complain about the lack of variety in their rations. Despite having been fed miraculously by God's daily gift of manna ever since their travels began in Exodus 16, God's people are looking back to their time of slavery and servitude, and forgetting all that God had done for them. God has acted not only in rescuing them, but also in carrying his people this far as tenderly as a mother carries a nursing infant, supplying all their needs, as well as making himself known to them in a unique and unprecedented way.

He has been their God, desiring that they would be his people.

The way in which God fed his people through the wilderness years should have taught them to trust the rightness, and goodness, of their mission in God – which was to set out and follow him, leaving everything of Egypt and their old lives behind. God blessed their journey of faith with material provision and sustenance. This, in turn, teaches us to trust that God will provide all we need as we follow him, even in difficult and trying circumstances.

But we must not be like the example we are given here; that which God supplies is more than sufficient for us, and we should learn to be grateful for it, and to give thanks not only with our lips, but in our lives.

God's provision for us is both physical and spiritual, as the two are linked inextricably, as are all the promises of God to his people in the Old Testament. God really does provide for all our needs, sometimes miraculously so, often providentially or according to the natural skills and giftings with which he has equipped us and his Church. All of these practical, or physical, blessings point to the greater spiritual blessings which he offers for those who will trust him.

Although, through the book of Numbers, God feeds his people with heavenly manna, now God feeds us spiritually with himself in the person of his Son. When we put our trust in Jesus, we choose to be sustained by him; we draw our energy from him; he nourishes us with himself. We feed on him spiritually.

Upon the cross, Jesus gave his flesh for the world by giving up his mortal life and, when we place our trust in what he accomplished there in his death, he feeds us. This is nowhere truer than in Holy Communion. There, in bread that is broken, like Jesus' body, and in wine poured out, like Jesus' blood, we participate by faith in his death; spiritually eating, or drawing sustenance, directly from him.

All our needs are met in Jesus as we journey through this wilderness with him. Let us not look back to Egypt and how things might be without him; instead let's trust his promises as we go forward towards the promised land with him.

For reflection

- Do you find it easy or difficult to trust in God's promises?
- When do you feel most nourished by Christ?

Prayer

Father, we thank you for the gift of Jesus Christ,
whose body given for us upon the cross is true spiritual food;
help us to receive all that he offers,
and to feast upon this banquet by faith,
that we may be sustained all the years of our wandering.
Amen.

15
Spirit

So Moses went out and told the people the words of the LORD; and he gathered seventy elders of the people, and placed them all around the tent. Then the LORD came down in the cloud and spoke to him, and took some of the spirit that was on him and put it on the seventy elders; and when the spirit rested upon them, they prophesied. But they did not do so again.

Two men remained in the camp, one named Eldad, and the other named Medad, and the spirit rested on them; they were among those registered, but they had not gone out to the tent, and so they prophesied in the camp. And a young man ran and told Moses, 'Eldad and Medad are prophesying in the camp.' And Joshua son of Nun, the assistant of Moses, one of his chosen men, said, 'My lord Moses, stop them!' But Moses said to him, 'Are you jealous for my sake? Would that all the LORD's people were prophets, and that the LORD would put his spirit on them!'
(Numbers 11:24–9)

Now there are varieties of gifts, but the same Spirit; and there are varieties of services, but the same Lord; and there are varieties of activities, but it is the same God who activates all of them in everyone. To each is given the manifestation of the Spirit for the common good. To one is given through the Spirit the utterance of wisdom, and to another the utterance of knowledge according to the same Spirit, to another faith by the same Spirit, to another gifts of healing by the one Spirit, to another the working of miracles, to another prophecy, to another the discernment of spirits, to another various kinds of tongues, to another the interpretation of tongues. All these are activated by one and the same Spirit, who allots to each one individually just as the Spirit chooses.
(1 Corinthians 12:4–11)

God's people need leadership as they journey through the wilderness. Moses recognises that, although the people have God as their leader and guide, nevertheless they also need human assistance – people who serve God by serving his people. To this end, God partners with people in the execution of his plans. Although God is the source of salvation, and the one who achieves all his ends and objectives by the strength of his own arm, still he condescends to share with human actors a part in the drama of salvation.

When God wants to achieve something in the world, so often he does so by the sending of his Spirit. As we read the Old Testament, we see the Holy Spirit at work in limited or temporary ways. We read about the Spirit that brings to life the spirits of men and women, strengthening them for service, and giving useful gifts in times of need. We see this very clearly in the gift of prophecy which is given to the leaders who were appointed to assist Moses.

Prophecy is a matter of speaking God's word, to God's people, in God's time. This word, which is timely and well directed, has the power to edify and build up – but it also has the power to rebuke and tear down. Its power comes from the Spirit which speaks the word. In John 6:63, Jesus says that his words are spirit and life.

When we come to the New Testament, we are introduced to the Holy Spirit in fuller and more direct ways. We come to understand that the Holy Spirit is a divine person, in the same way (and of the same substance) as both God the Father and God the Son, from whom the Spirit eternally proceeds. As the Spirit has always proceeded from the Father and the Son, in their eternal love, so in time and space the Spirit is sent to do the work of God in the world.

It is a simplification, but it is true, to say that when God wishes to make himself known, he does so by his Son; and when God wishes to do a work in the world, he does so by his Spirit.

The work of the Holy Spirit continues in the modern day; both in the Church, through the life and gifts he brings; and in the world, by the conviction that he brings. The gifts that he brings to the Church equip us so that we can partner with God, as he does the work of leading us through our wilderness.

For reflection

- How have you experienced the gifts of the Holy Spirit in your life?
- What gifts should your church be praying for?

Prayer

Holy Spirit, you are Lord the Giver of Life;
we thank you that, as you proceed from the Father and Son in eternity,
so now you are sent forth to do the work of God.
Come into our hearts, we pray, bringing all your gifts and fruit,
so that we may serve your will in this world.
Amen.

16
Humble

While they were at Hazeroth, Miriam and Aaron spoke against Moses because of the Cushite woman whom he had married (for he had indeed married a Cushite woman); and they said, 'Has the LORD spoken only through Moses? Has he not spoken through us also?' And the LORD heard it. Now the man Moses was very humble, more so than anyone else on the face of the earth. Suddenly the LORD said to Moses, Aaron, and Miriam, 'Come out, you three, to the tent of meeting.' So the three of them came out. Then the LORD came down in a pillar of cloud, and stood at the entrance of the tent, and called Aaron and Miriam; and they both came forward. And he said, 'Hear my words:

When there are prophets among you,
   I the LORD make myself known to them in visions;
   I speak to them in dreams.
Not so with my servant Moses;
   he is entrusted with all my house.
With him I speak face to face—clearly, not in riddles;
   and he beholds the form of the LORD.'
(Numbers 12:1–8)

'Come to me, all you that are weary and are carrying heavy burdens, and I will give you rest. Take my yoke upon you, and learn from me; for I am gentle and humble in heart, and you will find rest for your souls. For my yoke is easy, and my burden is light.'
(Matthew 11:28–30)

The wilderness teaches us humility; it does so by wearying us and laying burdens upon us for us to carry. For the ancient Israelites, those burdens were real and tangible; our burdens are often spiritual or figurative, but they are no less real or wearisome. Despite this, God wants us to thrive in the wilderness. This may seem impossible, but think of a cactus in full bloom – it is possible! It is impossible, however, to thrive if we abandon humility for selfish pride. Because to do so means to stop relying entirely on God to provide and to guide, turning instead to our own strength and ingenuity. Prideful arrogance, which exalts our own capabilities, which cuts us off from our neighbours, which isolates us and trains us not to ask for help, is a sure-fire way of meeting disaster – both in the wilderness and in life in general.

Conversely, humility trains us to own our own weaknesses, but also to be honest about our strengths; to engage our neighbours in love and service, and to accept service in turn. Humility is needed as we journey together though this wilderness. The Bible is full of exhortations to humility, full of references to the way in which God blesses humility, and full of examples of God resisting the prideful or arrogant.

The example of Moses' supreme humility (as ironic as it may seem to modern readers) highlights for us the contrast between the great honour bestowed upon Moses, and the integrated way in which he dwelled among the rest of God's people. Moses was not humble in that he stooped excessively low, but in that he did not exploit his exalted position.

This is true of Moses in a way that hints at the truth of Jesus' humility. In the wonderful Christ hymn of Philippians 2:5-8, we read that 'Christ Jesus,

> who, though he was in the form of God,
> > did not regard equality with God
> > as something to be exploited,
> but emptied himself,
> > taking the form of a slave,
> > being born in human likeness.
> And being found in human form,
> > he humbled himself
> > and became obedient to the point of death—
> > even death on a cross.

Jesus, more than Moses, has a unique and prestigious position. Although Moses had indeed occupied a special place in the history of God's self-revelation to Israel, Jesus is himself the object of that revelation. Although the word of God came to Moses, Jesus is himself the Word of God. Although Moses beheld the 'form of the LORD', Jesus was in the 'form of God'.

Moses' humility was worked out in his refusal to exploit his position as God's servant. Jesus' humility was worked out in his refusal to exploit his equality with God, and so he comes to us now, not exalted, but humble. He comes to us in our wilderness journey to share our burdens and give us rest. He comes to us that we might learn from him how to be truly humble.

For reflection

- Are you growing in humility, or growing in pride?
- Does your humility allow you to draw closer to God?

Prayer

Jesus, Lord of my life,
I pray that you would teach me your humility;
send your Spirit to do the work of bringing my life into peaceful submission to your word,
that I may find blessing, and be a blessing to all,
to the glory of the Father.
Amen.

Part 3

REVELATION AT KADESH (NUMBERS 13:1 – 19:22)

God's people arrive at the border of the promised land, having journeyed through the wilderness. But here disaster strikes, as the people rebel and refuse to take hold of the promises of God. Here God's people learn the seriousness of sin, the lasting effects of its consequences, but also the unyielding mercy and forgiveness of God.

This section of the story opens with a three-part drama, in which God's people scout out the land, return with a varied report, which leads to a full-blown rebellion. In this story, we learn about our human tendency to distrust God, to prefer sin over holiness and to focus on negativity. But we also learn about God's unchanging holiness, as well as the way in which God always brings his plans to fruition.

The third week in Lent

Monday: spies (Numbers 13:1–2, 21–4)
Tuesday: report (Numbers 13:25–33)
Wednesday: rebellion (Numbers 14:1–4)
Thursday: steadfast love (Numbers 14:11–18)
Friday: forgiveness (Numbers 14:20–5)
Saturday: fringes (Numbers 15:37–41)

17

Spies

The LORD said to Moses, 'Send men to spy out the land of Canaan, which I am giving to the Israelites; from each of their ancestral tribes you shall send a man, every one a leader among them.'

So they went up and spied out the land from the wilderness of Zin to Rehob, near Lebo-hamath. They went up into the Negeb, and came to Hebron; and Ahiman, Sheshai, and Talmai, the Anakites, were there. (Hebron was built seven years before Zoan in Egypt.) And they came to the Wadi Eshcol, and cut down from there a branch with a single cluster of grapes, and they carried it on a pole between two of them. They also brought some pomegranates and figs. That place was called the Wadi Eshcol, because of the cluster that the Israelites cut down from there.
(Numbers 13:1–2, 21–4)

Peter began to say to him, 'Look, we have left everything and followed you.' Jesus said, 'Truly I tell you, there is no one who has left house or brothers or sisters or mother or father or children or fields, for my sake and for the sake of the good news, who will not receive a hundredfold now in this age—houses, brothers and sisters, mothers and children, and fields, with persecutions—and in the age to come eternal life. But many who are first will be last, and the last will be first.'
(Mark 10:28–31)

Today's reading opens with God's people on the border of the promised land – they have made it through the wilderness, led by God's hand, and they are about to see the goodness of God's promises.

The promises of God are good, and they find partial fulfilment in the good things of this world which are ours to enjoy with thankful hearts. God has blessed the world with a natural order that produces abundantly more than enough to sustain life without destitution, hunger or need. The abundance of this world is ours to enjoy, so long as through it we find the one who gave the gift and give thanks to him.

In the story from Numbers, God's people are on the verge of taking possession of a good land, the attainment of which would fulfil the promises of God to their people. Once they have settled in it, that blessed land will enable them to live in such a way as to be a blessing to all the world. The mission of the spies is their first experience of it, and so here they get a foretaste of all the good things that God has in store for them. The great fecundity and fruitfulness of the land are described in wonderful pictorial language, with a single cluster of grapes being so large as to be carried by two men.

The question for the Israelites is whether they will trust God to bring them into ownership of the land. Can God be trusted to extend the blessing which he has placed upon his land to them, his people?

As we come to the New Testament, we move away from the temporal or earthly fulfilment of God's good promises to us, as our eyes move heavenwards. God's promises are still good, and indeed he still abundantly blesses us in this life, but we must ask ourselves how lightly we can hold these blessings. Having received blessings at God's hand, will we trust God enough to let them go? Will we fixate on the pomegranates, grapes and figs of the promised land and so lose sight of the giver of gifts who gave them in the first place?

As we shall see in the coming days, the abundance of blessing, both natural and supernatural, which God's people saw during this time in the wilderness – as they edged closer and closer to the promised land – would not be enough to hold them steadfast in God's service. The wilderness teaches us that, until we can seek God for himself in the absence of his temporal or earthly blessings, we will not be willing to seek God for himself even for all the figs in the world.

For reflection

- How has God blessed you materially?
- Are you able to use those blessings to bless others?

Prayer

God of all goodness,
I thank you that you have lavished your gifts upon the world;
continue your generosity, I pray.

Teach me gratitude and thankfulness,
so that I can fix my eyes on the future fulfilment of all your good promises
through Jesus Christ my Lord.
Amen.

18
Report

At the end of forty days they returned from spying out the land. And they came to Moses and Aaron and to all the congregation of the Israelites in the wilderness of Paran, at Kadesh; they brought back word to them and to all the congregation, and showed them the fruit of the land. And they told him, 'We came to the land to which you sent us; it flows with milk and honey, and this is its fruit. Yet the people who live in the land are strong, and the towns are fortified and very large; and besides, we saw the descendants of Anak there. The Amalekites live in the land of the Negeb; the Hittites, the Jebusites, and the Amorites live in the hill country; and the Canaanites live by the sea, and along the Jordan.'

But Caleb quieted the people before Moses, and said, 'Let us go up at once and occupy it, for we are well able to overcome it.' Then the men who had gone up with him said, 'We are not able to go up against this people, for they are stronger than we.' So they brought to the Israelites an unfavourable report of the land that they had spied out, saying, 'The land that we have gone through as spies is a land that devours its inhabitants; and all the people that we saw in it are of great size. There we saw the Nephilim (the Anakites come from the Nephilim); and to ourselves we seemed like grasshoppers, and so we seemed to them.'
(Numbers 13:25–33)

Who will separate us from the love of Christ? Will hardship, or distress, or persecution, or famine, or nakedness, or peril, or sword? As it is written,

'For your sake we are being killed all day long;
     we are accounted as sheep to be slaughtered.'

No, in all these things we are more than conquerors through him who loved us. For I am convinced that neither death, nor life, nor angels, nor rulers, nor things present, nor things to come, nor powers, nor height, nor depth, nor anything else in all creation, will be able to separate us from the love of God in Christ Jesus our Lord. (Romans 8:35–9)

We often like to read stories about people from history who snatched victory from the jaws of defeat – but being a person who supports both the England football team and Tottenham Hotspur, I have had to grow accustomed to the opposite: coming within touching distance of a win, only to 'snatch defeat from the jaws of victory'. Whether through lack of skill, over-confidence or an honest mistake, so often in life we lose our reward, just at the moment when we should be claiming it.

In our reading from Numbers, the people of God lose their reward because, despite the goodness of God which they have already experienced, they cannot find it within themselves to trust God's promise to them.

The storytelling continues in full flow from where we left off yesterday. The spies have returned from searching out the land, but they offer a varied report. The majority of the spies decry the plan to seize the land; they do not trust that God who has safely brought them this far will make good on his promise of the gift of land. They cannot escape their fears, which have clung to them all along the journey. They keep returning to the pernicious fear that they have left all they knew in slavery in Egypt for nothing. Their fear of death is greater than their trust in God.

As Christians, we must learn to trust God. As the hymn puts it,

There's no other way
to be happy in Jesus,
but to trust and obey.[1]

The trust that we place in God to fulfil his promises to us works itself out in our obedience to his word; but it also shapes our perceptions of the problems that we face, the solutions that seem open to us, and the way we talk about our situation.

---

1 J. H. Sammis, 'Trust and Obey'.

Most of the spies did not trust, because they did not have faith, and this led them to perceive problems rather than opportunities; to doubt the solutions which God had already promised; and to report back with fearfulness and doubt.

As we persevere through our own wilderness journey, we need to trust like Caleb did. This trust in the love of Christ that makes us more than conquerors will radically change our outlook. We will be able to see that God will overcome our problems; we will find new and exciting solutions which we could not have imagined; and the way that we talk about our situation – our report – will shift from negativity to positivity.

As we move through our wilderness journey, we must keep our faith fixed firmly on the love of Christ as it transforms us into people who trust God to fulfil his promises for us. We must watch as we make our way towards our promised land that we don't fail to trust God, and so snatch defeat from the jaws of victory.

For reflection

- Have you ever failed a challenge when you were close to its end?
- What have you learned from some of your failures?

Prayer

I call to you, LORD, come quickly to me . . .
may my prayer be set before you like incense . . .
Set a guard over my mouth, LORD;
keep watch over the door of my lips.
Do not let my heart be drawn to what is evil
so that I take part in wicked deeds . . .
Fix my eyes on you, Sovereign LORD;
so that in you I take refuge.
(Psalm 141:1–4, 8, NIV, adapted)

19

Rebellion

Then all the congregation raised a loud cry, and the people wept that night. And all the Israelites complained against Moses and Aaron; the whole congregation said to them, 'Would that we had died in the land of Egypt! Or would that we had died in this wilderness! Why is the LORD bringing us into this land to fall by the sword? Our wives and our little ones will become booty; would it not be better for us to go back to Egypt?' So they said to one another, 'Let us choose a captain, and go back to Egypt.'
(Numbers 14:1–4)

As they were going along the road, someone said to him, 'I will follow you wherever you go.' And Jesus said to him, 'Foxes have holes, and birds of the air have nests; but the Son of Man has nowhere to lay his head.' To another he said, 'Follow me.' But he said, 'Lord, first let me go and bury my father.' But Jesus said to him, 'Let the dead bury their own dead; but as for you, go and proclaim the kingdom of God.' Another said, 'I will follow you, Lord; but let me first say farewell to those at my home.' Jesus said to him, 'No one who puts a hand to the plough and looks back is fit for the kingdom of God.'
(Luke 9:57–62)

In music, a crescendo is where the song or piece builds and builds to a great climactic moment. The story of the wilderness journey so far has been building to this climax. God's people have reached the promised land. It is time for them to take possession of it but, rather than a sweet melodic climax, we encounter a cacophony of discordant cries of rebellion. God's people have come this far only to reject God, reject his promises and reject the salvation that he won for them.

Their rejection of God has entailed a rejection of the leaders whom God had appointed for them, and a rejection of the word that God had spoken to them. In this moment they break faith entirely, renouncing their words of promise made at Mount Sinai when they had acquiesced to the law of God in the giving of the Ten Commandments. This is apostasy, a rejection of faith once sincerely held, and it is borne out in the desire to return to slavery in Egypt.

The people have a lack of vision, insofar as they cannot see that which is so close; namely the fulfilment of all of God's promises to them. All they can now picture is the life they once lived in Egypt, albeit with rose-tinted spectacles. Psychologists sometimes refer to *euphoric recollection*, which is the tendency to remember something in a much more positive light than the lived experience actually deserves. Many of us will have done this with jobs, or relationships, on which we look back fondly – until someone reminds us of the reasons we left.

The Israelites have had plenty of opportunities to be reminded of the reasons why they left Egypt. Not just the negative reasons for wanting to escape slavery, but the positive reasons to go forward, which were rooted in the promises of God. So often in our own life we will feel a call backwards. This is a desire to abandon our spiritual journey through this wilderness and return to what we remember as the relative comfort of whatever Egypt we had left behind.

The Scriptures are full of exhortations not to look back; whether it is the story of Lot's wife in Genesis, famously turned into a pillar of salt; or the reminder in Proverbs that, as a dog returns to its vomit, so a fool returns to his folly. Jesus tells us that we must not look back. It is not that there is something sinful about the mechanics of looking backwards, but rather that looking back demonstrates where our hopes lie.

Do our hopes lie behind, in Egypt, which is slavery to sin, and certain death? Or do they lie ahead, across the waters of baptism, in the promised land, which is life everlasting in the kingdom of God?

For reflection

- Are you prone to looking back to old relationships, jobs or activities?
- In which ways can you keep looking forward instead?

Prayer

Almighty God, who made blind eyes see,
keep our focus upon you, and help us not to look back,

so that we may take hold of all your promises to us,
through Jesus Christ our Lord.
Amen.

20

Steadfast love

And the LORD said to Moses, 'How long will this people despise me? And how long will they refuse to believe in me, in spite of all the signs that I have done among them? I will strike them with pestilence and disinherit them, and I will make of you a nation greater and mightier than they.'

But Moses said to the LORD, 'Then the Egyptians will hear of it, for in your might you brought up this people from among them, and they will tell the inhabitants of this land. They have heard that you, O LORD, are in the midst of this people; for you, O LORD, are seen face to face, and your cloud stands over them and you go in front of them, in a pillar of cloud by day and in a pillar of fire by night. Now if you kill this people all at one time, then the nations who have heard about you will say, "It is because the LORD was not able to bring this people into the land he swore to give them that he has slaughtered them in the wilderness." And now, therefore, let the power of the LORD be great in the way that you promised when you spoke, saying,

> "The Lord is slow to anger,
> and abounding in steadfast love,
> forgiving iniquity and transgression,
> but by no means clearing the guilty,
> visiting the iniquity of the parents upon the children
> to the third and the fourth generation."'

(Numbers 14:11–18)

'You have heard that it was said, "You shall love your neighbour and hate your enemy." But I say to you, Love your enemies and pray for those who persecute you, so that you may be children of your Father

in heaven; for he makes his sun rise on the evil and on the good, and sends rain on the righteous and on the unrighteous.'
(Matthew 5:43–5)

A good friend of mine is a keen participant in amateur dramatics. She has performed in a number of low-cost productions in the theatre near where she lives. She is, humorously, atrocious. Often, she will need someone in the wings to feed her a line to help her remember what her character should say. Sometimes, when we read the Old Testament, it can appear as if this is going on. God has, seemingly, forgotten that he is loving – and Moses needs to remind him.

This is a particular storytelling device which we find frequently in the Hebrew Bible; but nowhere do we get the impression that the author, or those who first heard the words, really thought that God had forgotten what he is like.

God does not forget his character. The powerful storytelling at work in this, and similar, passages teaches us a wonderful way of praying; it is one that we can employ during our own wilderness experiences. We find examples of it throughout the Old Testament, especially in the Psalms. We also find it in many collect prayers, which tend to begin by addressing God as the God who acts in certain ways. It is a cry to God that he would remember his loving-kindness and act in mercy.

Of course, God doesn't need reminding – or his arm twisting – but we do. God's love is poured into our hearts abundantly (cf. Romans 5:5), even when it is not evident to us in the difficulties and challenges of this wilderness life.

God loves us with a steadfast and unending love, and he wants us to live in this love and to extend it to others. We must show this love even to our enemies, because that is what God does. In our readings from Numbers, God's people have betrayed him and their promises to him. They have rejected his leadership and the authority of those he has appointed for their good. They have come as far as the border of the promised land, only to insist on turning round again.

And yet, God does not let go. The story pictures it for us, with Moses 'reminding God' what he is really like. It is we who need reminding rather than God. Whenever we fear that God has abandoned or rejected us, because of the circumstances that assail us in our wilderness journey, we should cry out, 'Remember what you promised' – not because it will remind God, but because it forces us to put our trust in the promises of his word.

God promises to forgive us our sins, although I hasten to add that he does not promise us an escape from the natural consequences of our actions. His promise, both in word and precedent, is to show love even to his enemies. In the Old Testament, this is borne out by God's unceasing love for his people, even when they betray and abandon him in the wilderness. In the New Testament, this love for his enemies takes flesh and blood in the person of Jesus Christ. Jesus, who died for us even when we were at enmity with him in our hearts, is the steadfast love of the Lord that forgives all our sins – even our rebellion in the wilderness.

For reflection

- Do you find it helpful to cling to God's promises when you pray?
- Has God ever let you freely choose sin over righteousness?

Prayer

Father, help me to know your steadfast love;
let it change me, turn me, shape me,
until I am so enveloped by your care
that I never forget the promises you make through Jesus,
but trust them in the power of your Spirit.
Amen.

21
Forgiveness

Then the LORD said, 'I do forgive, just as you have asked; nevertheless—as I live, and as all the earth shall be filled with the glory of the LORD—none of the people who have seen my glory and the signs that I did in Egypt and in the wilderness, and yet have tested me these ten times and have not obeyed my voice, shall see the land that I swore to give to their ancestors; none of those who despised me shall see it. But my servant Caleb, because he has a different spirit and has followed me wholeheartedly, I will bring into the land into which he went, and his descendants shall possess it. Now, since the Amalekites and the Canaanites live in the valleys, turn tomorrow and set out for the wilderness by the way to the Red Sea.'
(Numbers 14:20–5)

Jesus said to his disciples, 'Occasions for stumbling are bound to come, but woe to anyone by whom they come! It would be better for you if a millstone were hung around your neck and you were thrown into the sea than for you to cause one of these little ones to stumble. Be on your guard! If another disciple sins, you must rebuke the offender, and if there is repentance, you must forgive. And if the same person sins against you seven times a day, and turns back to you seven times and says, "I repent", you must forgive.'
(Luke 17:1–4)

Forgiveness is hard. We might even say that it can feel unnatural, as though it goes against something inside us that wants to cling on to past hurts, even after our life has moved on to new territory. We cannot keep these resentments as we move from the wilderness to the promised land, and so the wilderness must become a time of shedding these burdens. Christians have learned that, in order to forgive, they must first learn to rely on the grace of the Holy Spirit, who works to make us more like Jesus. As we grow more and more like Jesus, it becomes more and more natural for us to forgive.

Jesus makes us more forgiving because he is forgiving. In Luke 23:34, we read his prayer as he is being crucified, 'Father, forgive them; for they do not know what they are doing.' This compassion and mercy is true of the person of Jesus as it is true for God in all eternity. Forgiveness is a divine trait, and to practice it not only makes us more like God, but also speaks of the way in which God has already made us to be like him.

At its most basic, forgiveness is a letting go. It is the letting go of grudges, letting go of a desire for vengeance, and a letting go of a requirement of retribution. Forgiveness truly is setting the prisoner free; but, in the process, we often discover that we ourselves were in fact the prison. Refusal to forgive frequently keeps us captive, embittered and chained to past hurts, much more than it does the one against whom we hold our grudge. Forgiveness is not something that we can demand of another person; we do not have the authority or moral standing to require that a hurting person forgives, in the way that Jesus so boldly can. We must never make Jesus' command to forgive, which is for the common good, into a weapon to beat the hurting and vulnerable.

Neither does Jesus require that we forgive recklessly those who do not repent and turn from their ways. We may choose to forgive in these circumstances, but that is our gift to give, both to ourselves and the one who wronged us. Moreover, forgiveness does not mean an abdication of justice; indeed true Christian justice is merciful. Throughout the Bible, we discover that, even when divine mercy and forgiveness remits sin and restrains the devastation that sin entails, nevertheless natural consequences follow. We see this in the story from Numbers. God's people have rebelled against him, and he swiftly puts down the rebellion – but, rather than acting as a despot and destroying entirely those who rebelled, he forgives. They cannot possess the great gift that would have been theirs by faith, but neither do they immediately receive the full payment for their distrust and rebellion in the wilderness.

Likewise, in our wilderness wanderings, we can be certain that God is quick to forgive us when we turn to him, and that he will give us good rewards as we journey with him. But we cannot hope to evade the temporal or earthly consequences of our actions, as though how we live or treat one another is unimportant.

For reflection

- Are you living with the natural consequences of any particular sin, either your own or someone else's?
- Is there anyone in your life whom you find it hard to forgive? Pray for them now.

Prayer

Father, help me to know you as the God who forgives,
give me grace to find forgiveness in your Son, Jesus Christ,
and fill me with your Spirit, that I may live forgiving others, as you have forgiven me.
Amen.

22
Fringes

The LORD said to Moses: Speak to the Israelites, and tell them to make fringes on the corners of their garments throughout their generations and to put a blue cord on the fringe at each corner. You have the fringe so that, when you see it, you will remember all the commandments of the LORD and do them, and not follow the lust of your own heart and your own eyes. So you shall remember and do all my commandments, and you shall be holy to your God. I am the LORD your God, who brought you out of the land of Egypt, to be your God: I am the LORD your God.
(Numbers 15:37–41)

As he went, the crowds pressed in on him. Now there was a woman who had been suffering from haemorrhages for twelve years; and though she had spent all she had on physicians, no one could cure her. She came up behind him and touched the fringe of his clothes, and immediately her haemorrhage stopped. Then Jesus asked, 'Who touched me?' When all denied it, Peter said, 'Master, the crowds surround you and press in on you.' But Jesus said, 'Someone touched me; for I noticed that power had gone out from me.' When the woman saw that she could not remain hidden, she came trembling; and falling down before him, she declared in the presence of all the people why she had touched him, and how she had been immediately healed. He said to her, 'Daughter, your faith has made you well; go in peace.'
(Luke 8:42b–48)

This week, we have been looking at one of most formative narrative events experienced by God's people in the Bible. We have heard many voices calling out: in rebellion and in submission, in despair and in hope, in anger and in forgiveness. These voices have caused quite a lot of noise, but now as the climactic crescendo of the last section of the wilderness journey quietens, the rebellion stalled, the people chastened yet forgiven, we hear God speak once more.

What God has to say to his people as they face their exile in the wilderness may, at first glance, seem strange or trifling – but his words are of enduring significance as we progress on our journey through this life. Fresh from their rebellion at the border of the promised land, the people receive a command from God instructing them to wear special fringes on the corners of their garments. But these fringes are not simply decorative. They are to remind the people of God's enduring presence, both in the midst of the wilderness journey, and then later when they enter the promised land.

God is not, of course, present in special clothing; but he is present, made known and encountered through his word. This is why it is so essential that the people do not forget the commands of the Lord their God. These commands are not merely examples of moral instruction, they are laws that point to the lawgiver: they reveal something of who God is. Biblical ethics grow out of the fact that God has made and ordered the universe in such a way that it echoes with his own moral nature.

When the woman in our Gospel reading reaches out, she reaches out both with faith in the promises of God and with remembrance of his commands. We do not have Jesus with us physically, and so we are unable to reach out and touch the fringe of his robe. We can, however, reach out in faith. We can cling to him in trust, as we remember the promises and commands of his word.

The story of God and his people will teach us that we do not naturally remember God, neither his promises nor his commands. Tassels on their garments will not be enough to cause God's people to remember, but God, for his part, will not forget his people. He is in our midst. He speaks by his word, he is made known by his commands, and he works by the Holy Spirit to engrave his law upon our hearts. We do not have special tassels on the fringes of our clothes, but if we trust Jesus, we do have his Spirit dwelling with us all the days of our wilderness journey.

For reflection

- Do you have any special ways to remind yourself of the presence of God?
- How could you keep God's commands in your mind more often?

Prayer

Almighty God, we give you thanks that we hear you through your word; continue to speak to us, write your law on our hearts, and be known to us, so that we may carry your presence with us always.
Amen.

Part 4

FROM KADESH TO MOAB (NUMBERS 20:1 – 22:1)

God's people must now put the promised land behind them as they follow the command of God out into the wilderness. They will continue to suffer and doubt, and to experience the consequences of their actions. It is here that significant leading characters in the story begin to die, as the generation of unfaithful Israelites begins to pass away. Judgement is, however, never the final word – God shows his mercy and love to his people.

The fourth week in Lent

Monday: water (Numbers 20:2–13)
Tuesday: obstacles (Numbers 20:14–21)
Wednesday: death (Numbers 20:1, 22–9)
Thursday: judgement (Numbers 21:4–9)
Friday: singing (Numbers 21:10, 16–20)
Saturday: victory (Numbers 21:33 – 22:1)

23
Water

Now there was no water for the congregation; so they gathered together against Moses and against Aaron. The people quarrelled with Moses and said, 'Would that we had died when our kindred died before the LORD! Why have you brought the assembly of the LORD into this wilderness for us and our livestock to die here? Why have you brought us up out of Egypt, to bring us to this wretched place? It is no place for grain, or figs, or vines, or pomegranates; and there is no water to drink.' Then Moses and Aaron went away from the assembly to the entrance of the tent of meeting; they fell on their faces, and the glory of the LORD appeared to them. The LORD spoke to Moses, saying: Take the staff, and assemble the congregation, you and your brother Aaron, and command the rock before their eyes to yield its water. Thus you shall bring water out of the rock for them; thus you shall provide drink for the congregation and their livestock.

So Moses took the staff from before the LORD, as he had commanded him. Moses and Aaron gathered the assembly together before the rock, and he said to them, 'Listen, you rebels, shall we bring water for you out of this rock?' Then Moses lifted up his hand and struck the rock twice with his staff; water came out abundantly, and the congregation and their livestock drank. But the LORD said to Moses and Aaron, 'Because you did not trust in me, to show my holiness before the eyes of the Israelites, therefore you shall not bring this assembly into the land that I have given them.' These are the waters of Meribah, where the people of Israel quarrelled with the LORD, and by which he showed his holiness.
(Numbers 20:2–13)

On the last day of the festival, the great day, while Jesus was standing there, he cried out, 'Let anyone who is thirsty come to me, and let the one who believes in me drink. As the scripture has said, "Out of the believer's heart shall flow rivers of living water."' Now he said this about the Spirit, which believers in him were to receive; for as yet there was no Spirit, because Jesus was not yet glorified. (John 7:37–9)

It has been joked that, since human beings are 70 per cent water, we are basically 'cucumbers with anxiety'. God's people are anxious once again in our story from Numbers, as the pattern of doubt, rebellion, judgement and mercy continues to repeat itself. We might have thought that they would have learned their lesson by now. Perhaps we are brave enough, or foolish enough, to assert that, if we were in their place, we would have put our anxieties behind us and trusted in God.

One of the lessons of this wilderness experience is that, when pressed by the material needs of the body, we do not naturally trust God.

Instead, our anxieties rise, and we cling on to God-given gifts as if they were ours by right, and come to doubt the generosity of God. The seemingly endless narrative cycles of doubt, rebellion, judgement and mercy that we encounter in these stories, condensed into a few short chapters, tell us a great deal about the grand sweep of our lives, and the recurrent patterns in which we too can be caught up.

But does it have to be like this? Can't we hope to escape the pattern laid down in the story of the wandering Israelites – and break the cycle of sin? The answer is 'Yes', but the breaking of this cycle of sin will not come from the strike of Moses' staff. The weight of the law of Moses alone cannot free us; it can only show us our captivity. We can see how Moses' powerful presence did not prevent the people from constant backsliding, so the law that he brought cannot be our catalyst for change either.

Whereas Moses gave the people water despite their sin and rebellion, Jesus causes to well up within us a spring of water that quenches the flame of sin and the thirst for rebellion. Jesus is able to break the seemingly endless cycle of doubt, rebellion, judgement and mercy by giving us his Spirit to drink. As he tells the woman at the well in John 4:14 (NIV), 'whoever drinks the water I give them will never thirst'.

This is an answer to the perpetual cry of the wilderness, where water is so scarce; God not only provides, but will give us a will and a desire to pursue his good gifts according to the purposes and patterns he has established in his word. God does this by his gift of the Holy Spirit, by which we are born again through the waters of baptism.

We may sometimes still find ourselves to be 'cucumbers with anxiety', but if we have the gift of the Holy Spirit, we will learn to thirst no longer.

For reflection

- What makes you anxious?
- How can you offer these anxieties to God?

Prayer

Father, we are anxious all too often,
weighed down by the cares of this world.
Sometimes the concerns are legitimate,
sometimes they are of our own invention;
whatever the cause, you offer your Spirit to calm our hearts.
Amen.

24

Obstacles

Moses sent messengers from Kadesh to the king of Edom, 'Thus says your brother Israel: You know all the adversity that has befallen us: how our ancestors went down to Egypt, and we lived in Egypt a long time; and the Egyptians oppressed us and our ancestors; and when we cried to the LORD, he heard our voice, and sent an angel and brought us out of Egypt; and here we are in Kadesh, a town on the edge of your territory. Now let us pass through your land. We will not pass through field or vineyard, or drink water from any well; we will go along the King's Highway, not turning aside to the right hand or to the left until we have passed through your territory.'

But Edom said to him, 'You shall not pass through, or we will come out with the sword against you.' The Israelites said to him, 'We will stay on the highway; and if we drink of your water, we and our livestock, then we will pay for it. It is only a small matter; just let us pass through on foot.' But he said, 'You shall not pass through.' And Edom came out against them with a large force, heavily armed. Thus Edom refused to give Israel passage through their territory; so Israel turned away from them.
(Numbers 20:14–21)

Paul wanted Timothy to accompany him; and he took him and had him circumcised because of the Jews who were in those places, for they all knew that his father was a Greek. As they went from town to town, they delivered to them for observance the decisions that had been reached by the apostles and elders who were in Jerusalem. So the churches were strengthened in the faith and increased in numbers daily.

They went through the region of Phrygia and Galatia, having been forbidden by the Holy Spirit to speak the word in Asia. When they had come opposite Mysia, they attempted to go into Bithynia,

but the Spirit of Jesus did not allow them; so, passing by Mysia, they went down to Troas.
(Acts 16:3–8)

The classic children's book *We're Going on a Bear Hunt* by Michael Rosen is a fun story about perseverance through a range of obstacles that stand in the way of a family adventure. The characters are confronted with things that cannot be jumped over nor tunnelled under, but must be endured – causing lots of mess![1]

Whether it is long grass, oozy mud or something else that gets in the way, the moral is to persevere. This is a great starting point when considering our wilderness journey generally. We might not want to go through it, but we must.

There are, however, things in our life that we cannot just push on through. These are those difficulties that not only must be endured for a season, but which force us to change the course of our journey; sometimes in ways that we would never have chosen or even predicted.

Such obstacles might include bereavement, the breakdown of a relationship, being made redundant or failing to achieve our ambitions in work or in family life. There are an almost infinite number of variations on these or similar themes that present insurmountable obstacles. They are challenges that we cannot simply wade through, roadblocks that cause our journey to change direction.

Often, these times in our lives will be painful. So much of the pain that we experience comes from the attachment that we have to the future that we feel we have lost. Allowing ourselves to mourn our losses can help us in these most difficult times; so can trusting that we have not been abandoned by God. He is with us in the present moment of grief and is preparing a future for us which is real, attainable and good.

It might feel as if we are giving up, but sometimes we need to be sensitive to what the Spirit is saying to us. We should ask God, with an open mind and an attentive heart, if it is time for us to follow him down a path which we did not choose and into a future which we cannot predict. The way that lies before us may lead us back towards the wilderness, seemingly away from the earthly or temporal promises of blessing. During these times, we may feel further away from answered prayer than at any other time in our

---

1 M. Rosen, *We're Going on a Bear Hunt* (New York : Margaret K. McElderry, 2009).

wilderness wanderings, but we will not be further from God. If the Spirit of Jesus does not permit us to proceed in one direction, whether this is conveyed to us by providence or by inner conviction, then the same Spirit will go before us and come alongside us on the route that we must take.

For reflection

- What insurmountable obstacles have you encountered in your life or relationships?
- Have there been periods in your life when you have felt far from God?

Prayer

Loving Father, whose Son trod the path of pain and suffering,
make yourself known to me today,
so that, when I know I must turn away from the path I have been taking,
I will learn to trust your presence with me,
even when I cannot know the route ahead.
Amen.

25

Death

The Israelites, the whole congregation, came into the wilderness of Zin in the first month, and the people stayed in Kadesh. Miriam died there, and was buried there. . .

They set out from Kadesh, and the Israelites, the whole congregation, came to Mount Hor. Then the LORD said to Moses and Aaron at Mount Hor, on the border of the land of Edom, 'Let Aaron be gathered to his people. For he shall not enter the land that I have given to the Israelites, because you rebelled against my command at the waters of Meribah. Take Aaron and his son Eleazar, and bring them up Mount Hor; strip Aaron of his vestments, and put them on his son Eleazar. But Aaron shall be gathered to his people, and shall die there.' Moses did as the Lord had commanded; they went up Mount Hor in the sight of the whole congregation. Moses stripped Aaron of his vestments, and put them on his son Eleazar; and Aaron died there on the top of the mountain. Moses and Eleazar came down from the mountain. When all the congregation saw that Aaron had died, all the house of Israel mourned for Aaron thirty days.
(Numbers 20:1, 22–9)

But we do not want you to be uninformed, brothers and sisters, about those who have died, so that you may not grieve as others do who have no hope. For since we believe that Jesus died and rose again, even so, through Jesus, God will bring with him those who have died.
(1 Thessalonians 4:13–15)

All of us will know someone who has died. Going through the process of losing loved ones to death is part of growing up, and none of us will escape the touch of grief. Perhaps you will recall especially the first time a close relative or friend died after you had reached an age where you could understand and be affected by the death. No doubt it was painful in a new and profound way. I can recall losing my grandmother when I was very small. I was big enough to understand that I wouldn't see her again, but I was still too small really to understand what had happened. This had all changed by the time my grandfather died, some years later. Bereavement now meant something to me.

It is not an exaggeration to say that everyone we know will, one day, die; and so will we. We don't like to think about it. Some of us were taught not to talk about it. The modern world has been remarkably good at hiding it away from our eyes, with a great many deaths taking place away from home, in hospitals and hospices, with professionals rather than family in attendance. If we are not careful, this can enable us to pretend it isn't going to happen, that we might evade grief and death. This sort of denial only leads to greater devastation.

The latter time of wilderness wanderings that God's people endured was, in one sense, a death sentence. They were exiled from their hope of entering the promised land and were to die in the wilderness. This is an echo, or a microcosm, of the story of our first parents, Adam and Eve. They rebelled against the good and gentle rule of God, condemning themselves to death. Exiled from Eden, they were cast out into the wilderness of the world until such a time as their bodies should return to the dust from which they had been taken.

The grand narrative of the whole of human history follows this pattern, too. We find ourselves journeying through the wilderness all the days of our mortal life. We follow in the footsteps of Adam and Eve and all of God's people, as we await the day our bodies return to the earth, while always longing for an eternal home – longing for the promised land.

In Jesus Christ, this hope, this longing, becomes a certain reality. He alone has beaten this wilderness experience, having passed through it spotless and without blemish. Dying his people's death upon the cross, he has put death to death. And by rising to life again, he is able to bring us with him. Jesus' body has been raised glorious and eternal. He has become both the means of attaining entrance to the promised land and also the first fruits of its life. So now, when we face death, we can do so with hope.

The wilderness ceases to be simply a death sentence for God's people, but instead becomes the place of preparation where we are made ready for our eternal home.

For reflection

- Has death been a major part of your life?
- How do you cope when someone you know has died?

Prayer

Father, we thank you that, because of Christ's death,
death itself is a defeated enemy;
give us grace to know that, through faith in him,
we can live with you for ever.
Amen.

26
Judgement

From Mount Hor they set out by the way to the Red Sea, to go around the land of Edom; but the people became impatient on the way. The people spoke against God and against Moses, 'Why have you brought us up out of Egypt to die in the wilderness? For there is no food and no water, and we detest this miserable food.' Then the LORD sent poisonous serpents among the people, and they bit the people, so that many Israelites died. The people came to Moses and said, 'We have sinned by speaking against the LORD and against you; pray to the LORD to take away the serpents from us.' So Moses prayed for the people. And the LORD said to Moses, 'Make a poisonous serpent, and set it on a pole; and everyone who is bitten shall look at it and live.' So Moses made a serpent of bronze, and put it upon a pole; and whenever a serpent bit someone, that person would look at the serpent of bronze and live.
(Numbers 21:4–9)

'If I have told you about earthly things and you do not believe, how can you believe if I tell you about heavenly things? No one has ascended into heaven except the one who descended from heaven, the Son of Man. And just as Moses lifted up the serpent in the wilderness, so must the Son of Man be lifted up, that whoever believes in him may have eternal life.'
(John 3:12–15)

As I sit writing this, I have a sore arm from a Covid booster shot. A good friend of mine works in pharmaceuticals, and she has been trying to explain to me how many modern medicines work – *trying* being the operative word, because I was never any good at science. I understand that the solution to a medical problem often lies in the problem itself. So, with vaccines, doctors give you part of the virus in order to stimulate your immune response. Similarly, an antidote is part of a poison used to heal us from the poison that has harmed us. There is something like this happening in our reading from Numbers.

We begin with God's people once again rejecting the goodness of God's salvation. They are looking back to slavery in Egypt rather than looking forward to entering the promised land with God. They complain to God, grumbling about the freedom that God has won for them. Their rejection of their own salvation, their looking back rather than looking forward, has led to God giving the people over to judgement, which comes in the form of venomous serpents.

Crucially, judgement is not the final word. Rather, it is the context for God to act in mercy. God doesn't call off the judgement, which hung heavily over his people for their disobedience. Nor does God ignore his people's sin, as though how people behave towards and think about God is of no importance. No; but, in the midst of judgement, God appoints a means for his people to be saved.

God gives them a way through; and this, for them, is to look at the bronze snake as it is lifted up in the wilderness. We can learn from their experience how God makes a way of mercy through the midst of judgement for those who look with faith. As I said, it's a bit like the way an antidote takes part of a poison to protect us from the poison; if an Israelite, once bitten by a venomous snake, looks up at the bronze snake, they will be saved. It might seem bizarre to us at first, but there is something very powerful going on.

If the Israelites hope to escape judgement, they must look at the image, or the representation, of the very judgement they hope to escape. They must look and live. Some fifteen hundred years later, when talking about the sort of faith that we must have, Jesus takes us to this story.

He says, 'just as Moses lifted up the snake in the wilderness, so the Son of Man must be lifted up, that everyone who believes may have eternal life in him' (John 3:14–15, NIV).

We are God's people. At first that sounds lovely, until we realise what God's people were like throughout the Bible: grumbling and sick with sin; prone to looking back to the slavery of sin, rather than looking forward to the promises of God. By recognising the similarity between us and the people of old, we come to understand that we share the same problem. And the heart of the human problem is the problem of the human heart.

But God in his mercy has devised a cure. A way has been made through the judgement that we all face. If we are God's people in this story, then Jesus, lifted up upon the cross, is the bronze snake lifted up in the wilderness. Behold the one lifted up. Look and live. Do not look back to your old lives of slavery to sin, but look up to the cross where Jesus becomes the very thing that afflicted us – according to 2 Corinthians 5:21, 'for our sake he made him to be sin who knew no sin, so that in him we might become the righteousness of God'.

What must we do? We must look and live – it is the only cure. We cannot try to suck out the poison, we cannot try to make an offering to appease God, we certainly cannot ignore the wound – no, we must look to the cross and live.

For reflection
- Does God still execute his judgement in the world?
- In what ways is judgement the context for mercy?

Prayer
Almighty God, your judgement is just and your saving love is merciful; teach me to see in your will both righteousness and grace, so that I can come to understand the saving power of the cross. Amen.

27
Singing

The Israelites set out, and camped in Oboth... From there they continued to Beer; that is the well of which the LORD said to Moses, 'Gather the people together, and I will give them water.' Then Israel sang this song:

> 'Spring up, O well!—Sing to it!—
> the well that the leaders sank,
> that the nobles of the people dug,
> with the sceptre, with the staff.'

From the wilderness to Mattanah, from Mattanah to Nahaliel, from Nahaliel to Bamoth, and from Bamoth to the valley lying in the region of Moab by the top of Pisgah that overlooks the waste-land. (Numbers 21:10, 16–20)

Do not get drunk with wine, for that is debauchery; but be filled with the Spirit, as you sing psalms and hymns and spiritual songs among yourselves, singing and making melody to the Lord in your hearts, giving thanks to God the Father at all times and for everything in the name of our Lord Jesus Christ. (Ephesians 5:18–20)

It has been around twenty years since I attended my first rock concert. Although, in the intervening time, I have come to prefer other forms of musical performance, I can still remember very vividly the sensation of being in a large group of my peers singing at the top of my lungs. Participating in large musical events can be deeply moving; some people even describe such concerts or festivals in spiritual terms. It doesn't surprise me at all that some of us will find such concerts overwhelming, as they can be disorientating as well as exhilarating. Singing, especially in groups, can touch a deep part of us.

Singing in British churches was, sadly, banned for months on end as a precaution during the coronavirus pandemic. The way we worshipped during that period, whether in words or silence, has led me to reflect on how worship must be experienced by Christians who are never free to sing in public, whether that is because they are prisoners, or because they live in isolation or in countries closed to the gospel. Perhaps that time should have been an encouragement for us to pray for people in such situations. For many of us, church without singing was just not the same. Singing enables us to harmonise spiritually, as we join our voices together audibly. Churches that give preference to excellent sung worship, in whatever style or context, tend in my experience to draw a crowd. No doubt this is in part because such singing is entertaining; but I also suspect that it engenders sensations which we could recognise as spiritual experiences.

In our reading from Numbers, God's people are marking a time in their life together, and a particular place in their journey as a community, with a song. The Old Testament is littered with songs, and the book of Psalms is something of a songbook with 150 songs telling the story of God and his people. At many major turning points, both positive and negative, there is a song – songs of rejoicing, songs of lament, songs that gather the thoughts, hopes and feelings of God's people into one voice.

In a similar way, the Church uses thematic hymns to mark the passing seasons of the liturgical year. We can think of the emotional weight that certain Christmas carols might hold for us, as they bring back and make real in the moment our memories of childhood Christmases. For example, I can't sing 'In the Bleak Midwinter' without being transported back to my primary school's annual carol service.

Since we are God's people, spiritual songs can act as points of reference and landmarks along our journey of faith, as we make our way through the wilderness of this life. We may have particular hymns that correspond in our minds and hearts with significant life events, such as weddings or funerals, or we may treasure a special song that was meaningful to us at a specific time or season of our life.

I was glad when singing returned to our churches. Even wearing a mask, I felt that something fresh and new had enlivened my experience of worship, which had been sustained only by the spoken word for so long. St Augustine is believed to have said, 'The one who sings prays twice', and moving from purely spoken worship to worship with singing is something like moving from black-and-white television to colour. I hope that we cling fast to our songs, and I hope that the Church continues to compose new songs that reflect our changing lives and locations along this wilderness journey.

For reflection
- What are some of your favourite hymns, and why?
- What sort of music do you most enjoy listening to, and should that music find a place in church?

Prayer
Anoint my voice, Lord, with the seal of your Spirit,
that I may praise your wonderful works,
and sing of your saving deeds.
Give me grace to tell out all that has been done for me through you,
O Christ.
Amen.

28
Victory

Then they turned and went up the road to Bashan; and King Og of Bashan came out against them, he and all his people, to battle at Edrei. But the LORD said to Moses, 'Do not be afraid of him; for I have given him into your hand, with all his people, and all his land. You shall do to him as you did to King Sihon of the Amorites, who ruled in Heshbon.' So they killed him, his sons, and all his people, until there was no survivor left; and they took possession of his land.

The Israelites set out, and camped in the plains of Moab across the Jordan from Jericho.
(Numbers 21:33 – 22:1)

For the love of God is this, that we obey his commandments. And his commandments are not burdensome, for whatever is born of God conquers the world. And this is the victory that conquers the world, our faith. Who is it that conquers the world but the one who believes that Jesus is the Son of God?
(1 John 5:3–5)

What does victory look like, and how would we know we have achieved it? In the epic drama *1917*, which recounts the story of a First World War messenger tasked with delivering a command to call off an ill-fated attack, we see a range of different visions of victory. On learning that many men might die, Colonel Mackenzie, who is in charge of the assault, tells his men that they must not pause for even a moment because the end is within sight. Later, he reflects that the war will continue until only one person is left to fight. Is the only victory we can imagine a victory where we are the only ones left? This is the victory present in today's reading from Numbers.

God's people are vulnerable, recently set free from oppression and harassed by attacking armies on all sides. In our reading, Og, the King of

Bashan, has come out against Israel as God's people have attempted to pass through the land. But Og is hoisted by his own petard, as his attempted destruction of the Israelites leads to his own destruction. The victory that the Israelites win here is a victory that frees them from certain threats and grants them certain liberties – but is not a lasting or eternal victory.

Although Og is defeated here, and a reprieve of rest is granted to God's people, nevertheless the Israelites will continue to be beset by warring enemies bent on their obliteration. We see this lasting danger play out in the book of Judges and then the long history of the kings of Israel. So long as the victory in sight is military or to do with the defeat of human enemies, it cannot be lasting. The Bible teaches us that, if our idea of victory only conceives of it as the conquest of other peoples, then it will never be true or eternal.

A longer view of the Bible enables us to see God's great triumph over the forces of evil, over sin and death. This victory is not won by force of might or by human strength, but in weakness and shame. God's great victory is won upon the cross of Christ, when the powers of evil in this world are defeated.

In our wilderness journey, we will come up against challenges; there will be those who set out to defeat us or push us back. When we strive for victory in our personal life, we must keep in mind that the threats we face are different from those faced by the people of God in the Old Testament. Nevertheless, we are required to challenge the spiritual realities that confront us. This is made explicit for us when Paul says in Ephesians 6:12, 'Our struggle is not against enemies of blood and flesh, but against the rulers, against the authorities, against the cosmic powers of this present darkness, against the spiritual forces of evil in the heavenly places.'

Accordingly, we must not see the world as being full of enemies to be defeated, but as full of people to be loved. In this way, we can grow as we place our trust in Jesus, who gives us the victory: our faith.

For reflection

- What victories has God won for you in your life?
- Does it make a difference to know that God is fighting for you?

Prayer

Almighty God, we give you thanks and praise
because you have won for us the victory,

through Jesus Christ your Son;
help us to live the truth of that victory
each and every day of lives
by the power of your Spirit.
Amen.

Part 5

REVELATION AT MOAB (NUMBERS 22:2 – 30:16)

The story of the wandering of God's people is drawing to a close. Many years spent in the wilderness are hastening by, as a new generation of God's people arises. They receive new laws that will prepare them for their occupation of the promised land. First, we meet some new characters and hear new narratives, which provide some fresh perspective on the relationship between God, his people and the promises that bind them together.

Fifth week in Lent
Monday: curses (Numbers 22:1–6)
Tuesday: blessings (Numbers 23:18–23)
Wednesday: sex (Numbers 25:1–3)
Thursday: fresh start (Numbers 26:1–4, 63–4)
Friday: Joshua (Numbers 27:12–20)
Saturday: offerings (Numbers 28:11–15)

29
Curses

The Israelites set out, and camped in the plains of Moab across the Jordan from Jericho. Now Balak son of Zippor saw all that Israel had done to the Amorites. Moab was in great dread of the people, because they were so numerous; Moab was overcome with fear of the people of Israel. And Moab said to the elders of Midian, 'This horde will now lick up all that is around us, as an ox licks up the grass of the field.' Now Balak son of Zippor was king of Moab at that time. He sent messengers to Balaam son of Beor at Pethor, which is on the Euphrates, in the land of Amaw, to summon him, saying, 'A people has come out of Egypt; they have spread over the face of the earth, and they have settled next to me. Come now, curse this people for me, since they are stronger than I; perhaps I shall be able to defeat them and drive them from the land; for I know that whomsoever you bless is blessed, and whomsoever you curse is cursed.'
(Numbers 22:1–6)

'But I say to you that listen, Love your enemies, do good to those who hate you, Bless those who curse you, pray for those who abuse you. If anyone strikes you on the cheek, offer the other also; and from anyone who takes away your coat do not withhold even your shirt.'
(Luke 6:27–9)

Envy, fear, prejudice, anger, hatred: the list of reasons why a person might curse another is long. It is very likely that anyone who feels compelled to curse another has experienced several of these motivating emotions all at once. In our reading from Numbers, Balak the king of Moab wishes to call down real and powerful curses upon God's people. Accordingly, he goes to entreat a local well-known prophet, Balaam. In those days, lots of people would ply their trade as prophets or seers, people who were believed to have some special connection to the divine. Our reading takes this assumption at face value, and so we meet Balaam as King Balak puts his faith in him.

Balaam is tasked with cursing God's people. This will be a pre-emptive strike, of sorts, in the days before drones could rain down missiles on unsuspecting enemies. King Balak wants to seize an early advantage, and avoid the fate of other neighbouring kingdoms, which have simply attacked Israel. It is expected that Balaam, with his secret knowledge of the spiritual realm, will be able to make binding pronouncements upon the enemies of Balak as they make their way through his territory towards the promised land.

The chances that someone will attempt to curse us using something like a formal curse or incantation as we make our wilderness journey through this life is probably pretty small. Although I am sure that, in certain contexts in the modern world, these sorts of practices may have continued or gained new popularity. It is more likely, in my experience, that we will encounter the cursing of people in our day-to-day lives by the use of negative, derogatory or abusive language We have all encountered blasphemy, even on television, which seeks to elicit tacit approval from us as we nod along with whatever appears on our screens.

The way we speak about one another is important. With our words, we shape our interaction with the world around us. Our words hold power far beyond simply communicating reality; they shape our perception of it and are part of the continuing creation of it. When we curse others, we shape how we, they and others perceive their places in the world, and we also shape their personal sense of worth. Moreover, we risk creating a negative spiritual climate which can have a profound effect on people.

When faced with cursing, Christians are called to speak a better word. Instead of returning curses for curses, we must speak words of love, of life and of blessing. To bless others with our words, and especially to bless those who curse us, means that we must encourage and build up. In Luke 6:28, Jesus clearly tells us, 'Bless those who curse you.'

For reflection

- Do you struggle to control what you say and how you speak about others?
- Do you need to repent of the way that you sometimes speak?

Prayer

Jesus, we thank you that upon the cross
you bore the full weight of the curse of sin
for us who trust you;
help us never to add to that burden,
or to curse others with our words or actions.
Amen.

30
Blessings

Then Balaam uttered his oracle, saying:

'Rise, Balak, and hear;
    listen to me, O son of Zippor:
God is not a human being, that he should lie,
    or a mortal, that he should change his mind.
Has he promised, and will he not do it?
    Has he spoken, and will he not fulfil it?
See, I received a command to bless;
    he has blessed, and I cannot revoke it.
He has not beheld misfortune in Jacob;
    nor has he seen trouble in Israel.
The LORD their God is with them,
    acclaimed as a king among them.
God, who brings them out of Egypt,
    is like the horns of a wild ox for them.
Surely there is no enchantment against Jacob,
    no divination against Israel;
now it shall be said of Jacob and Israel,
    "See what God has done!"'
(Numbers 23:18–23)

Then he began to speak, and taught them, saying:
'Blessed are the poor in spirit, for theirs is the kingdom of heaven.
'Blessed are those who mourn, for they will be comforted.
'Blessed are the meek, for they will inherit the earth.
'Blessed are those who hunger and thirst for righteousness, for they will be filled.
'Blessed are the merciful, for they will receive mercy.
'Blessed are the pure in heart, for they will see God.

'Blessed are the peacemakers, for they will be called children of
God.
'Blessed are those who are persecuted for righteousness' sake, for
theirs is the kingdom of heaven.'
(Matthew 5:2–10)

The earth is a blessed place. In the creation story, which we find in the
opening chapter of Genesis, we read that God blesses each fragment of his
created world. As he creates, he surveys the work in the order of its
completion and blesses it by proclaiming that it is 'good', and indeed 'very
good'. The world is good and has been made good by a good God. God
made it this way, ultimately, so that it can reflect his goodness; but part of
that work is done by it being a blessing to us who call this creation home.

We are blessed by its abundance, by its stability, by its goodness. Again,
this ultimately serves to point to the goodness of the creator, but it does
so by equipping us with all the material provisions we need to bless one
another. We are blessed so that we can be a blessing. This is practically a
universal rule of blessing in the Old Testament. For example, we can look
at the particular blessing that God promises to Abraham and his
descendants. In that story, it is made clear that this personal blessing is
not to be an end in itself, but it is to become the means of a general and
universal blessing. The blessing promised to one man, Abraham, reaches
its fullness in the blessings brought to all in Jesus Christ. Blessing gives
rise to blessing.

It is true, of course, that, although this world is blessed, it is also for
the time being under the curse of sin. For this reason, we must traverse the
wilderness that separates the Eden of Genesis blessings from the promised
land. We encounter brokenness whenever we encounter sin or its effects.
Ultimately, the wages of sin are death; but we feel its malevolent influence
whenever there is injustice or suffering. What is remarkable about the
teaching of Jesus is that he encourages us to see those who are victims or
survivors of the brokenness of this world – the hungry, the poor, the
oppressed – not as *people who have got what they deserve* but as *people who
can take hold of a special blessing from God* because they are in a unique
position of dependence on God as their king.

In our reading from Numbers, Balaam has refused to pronounce a
curse against God's people. He knows that such a curse would not, or
could not, be binding and effective, because it is contrary to the will and

purposes of God. Moreover, Balaam is given a word by God. This word, rather than cursing, is a declaration of blessing over Israel. It is a blessing that at its heart acknowledges the special way in which God is the king in the midst of his people. To have God as our king is to be blessed. To have God as our king is to be guarded, guided and governed by love itself. To have God as our king is to be loved. If we are blessed so that we might be a blessing, so we are loved that we in turn might love. God's redeeming action in the gospel is a word of blessing that enriches those who hear it and causes them to speak it afresh. The cross and resurrection of Christ is like a pebble thrown into the middle of a still pond, God's blessing of love and mercy ripples outwards by the overflowing of the Holy Spirit in our lives, our actions and our words.

For reflection
- In what ways has God blessed you?
- How can you share those blessings with others?

Prayer
Almighty God, from whom all good things come,
we give you thanks for all the blessings that you have poured on us.
Give us the wisdom to use those gifts for the glory of your name,
and for the good of your people,
that your blessing might go out into all the world.
Amen.

31
Sex

While Israel was staying at Shittim, the people began to have sexual relations with the women of Moab. These invited the people to the sacrifices of their gods, and the people ate and bowed down to their gods. Thus Israel yoked itself to the Baal of Peor, and the LORD's anger was kindled against Israel.
(Numbers 25:1–3)

'You have heard that it was said, "You shall not commit adultery." But I say to you that everyone who looks at a woman with lust has already committed adultery with her in his heart. If your right eye causes you to sin, tear it out and throw it away; it is better for you to lose one of your members than for your whole body to be thrown into hell.'
(Matthew 5:27–9)

The wilderness is a place of longing where many desires are left unfulfilled. Christians have long understood human desire in terms of appetites, both the root and the end of these being the desire for God. Appetites or desires for food and water speak to us of the life that we draw ultimately from God. It should be no surprise to us that Jesus talks about himself as being true food and offering living water. Our need for these things provides us with a lesson in our need of God.

The same is true of our sexual desire, which at its best points us to the human capacity for relationship, intimacy and love, all of which reflect the way that God made us in his image. Moreover, in a unique way among our appetites, sexual desire is linked to our capacity for procreation. It is through sex that we not only grow in love, intimacy and affection but are also able to make more humans – people made in the image of God.

Sex and sexual desire are part of God's good design for the world and for people. It is for this reason that, in the same way as the Old Testament paints the picture of the relationship between God and Israel as a marriage, the New Testament tells us that in marriage we discover a mystery that is about Christ and his Church. What we discover in our reading from Numbers is that sexual desire's power for good, if inverted, becomes a destructive force.

In the analogy we are given in the New Testament of Christ and his Church as the pattern for human sexual relationships, we come to understand just how vividly our sexual desires and behaviours display our beliefs about God and his world. If sex is to be an icon of Christ and his Church, then a misdirected sex life is a faulty icon, a feigned icon or an idol.

We see in our reading from Numbers the deep and pervasive link between immoral sex and idolatry. Not content with God's good design for sex and relationships, the men of Israel have followed unhealthy desires, and have tried to find fulfilment for their longings where it could not be found. A bigger issue than behaviour which the scripture condemns is, however, the question of the heart. God's people have seemingly endless misdirected desires, which they seek to be fulfilled in ways that God does not sanction.

We might think of the water from the rock or the quails in the wilderness, which were signs of God's merciful provision to a dissatisfied people, to help us see how God's people now abandon God's plan for sex and relationships as they look for a way to ease their dissatisfaction in Moab. This unwillingness to be content leads inexorably to pagan temple worship. The issue is the heart that desired such things, and the mind which thought that such desires could truly lead to fulfilment.

When Jesus tells us that a man who is in danger of lusting after a woman should gouge out his own eye if it causes him to sin (Matthew 5:28), he was in no sense encouraging self-mutilation. Fundamentally, it is not the eye that causes a man to lust, or the hand that causes a thief to steal; it is the heart. Jesus wants us to understand that we cannot find fulfilment for all our desires in this wilderness life, no matter how much we try. Instead, he tells us that we need new hearts so that we may know the first fruits of fulfilment, now in this present life, by the grace of the Holy Spirit.

For reflection

- Do you struggle with any unhealthy desires?
- Can we know the fulfilment of human desire in our union with God?

Prayer

Loving Lord, you have made us for yourself,
to desire you and take pleasure in you,
and our hearts are restless till they find their rest in you;
give us the rest which is the fulfilment of all desire,
the rest which is union with you.
Amen.
(Inspired by St Augustine of Hippo)

32
Fresh start

After the plague the LORD said to Moses and to Eleazar son of Aaron the priest, 'Take a census of the whole congregation of the Israelites, from twenty years old and upwards, by their ancestral houses, everyone in Israel able to go to war.' Moses and Eleazar the priest spoke with them in the plains of Moab by the Jordan opposite Jericho, saying, 'Take a census of the people, from twenty years old and upwards', as the LORD commanded Moses . . .

These were those enrolled by Moses and Eleazar the priest, who enrolled the Israelites in the plains of Moab by the Jordan opposite Jericho. Among these there was not one of those enrolled by Moses and Aaron the priest, who had enrolled the Israelites in the wilderness of Sinai.

(Numbers 26:1-4, 63-4)

When they had finished breakfast, Jesus said to Simon Peter, 'Simon son of John, do you love me more than these?' He said to him, 'Yes, Lord; you know that I love you.' Jesus said to him, 'Feed my lambs.' A second time he said to him, 'Simon son of John, do you love me?' He said to him, 'Yes, Lord; you know that I love you.' Jesus said to him, 'Tend my sheep.' He said to him the third time, 'Simon son of John, do you love me?' Peter felt hurt because he said to him the third time, 'Do you love me?' And he said to him, 'Lord, you know everything; you know that I love you.' Jesus said to him, 'Feed my sheep.'

(John 21:15-17)

'Cross it all out and start again' is a phrase that often preceded the scribbling out of a mistaken equation in my GCSE maths workbook. Sometimes, an error ran so deeply in my work that it couldn't be salvaged. Rather than being corrected, it needed to be forgotten and a fresh attempt made. The new start, a fresh attempt to get things right, can only be undertaken once the old attempt is out of the way. In our reading from Numbers, God has been in the process of crossing out the great act of rebellion that occasioned the permanent exile of his people.

The faithless generation has been living out a sentence of death, forbidden to enter the promised land, but all the while God has remained faithful to his promises. Although the people have surrendered their blessings, God is intent on blessing. Accordingly, we find the Israelites numbered for the second time in the book of Numbers. Whereas the men and women of the first census rebelled and bore the natural consequences of their sins, those enumerated here in Numbers 26 will take possession of the promises of God.

In this second census, God is sweeping away the reproach that lay over his people. Their time of punishment is ended: it was only temporary and it was the prelude to a great salvation. In the foregoing years, God's people were able to cross out all the rebellion and all the sin and start again. As Christians, we cling to the belief that, as much as God may need us to *cross out* in repentance our sinful working to date, he does not cross us out.

God is a God of second chances; he is a God of fresh starts and new beginnings. For every fall from grace and for every rebellion that we lead, we find an offer of reconciliation. We live and relive, every day of our lives, the pattern of forgiveness and restoration that we find in our reading from John. Jesus eats with Peter and restores him three times. Three times Peter is given the opportunity to affirm the love that he has for Jesus and undo the three betrayals that he has committed on the night of Jesus' trial.

Although Jesus prophesied that Peter would indeed betray him three times, he does not come with an 'I told you so'. Rather, Jesus offers Peter the same as he offers us: a chance to undo the betrayal. This second great census is Israel's chance to undo their betrayal and to put their trust in God. They will go on to sin again, but so will we. Yet we should give thanks that, if we return to him, God will enable us to persevere and will restore us.

For reflection

- What things in your life have you needed grace to cross out?
- Has God ever given you a second chance?

Prayer

Jesus, I thank you that you are the Lord of second chances.
Whenever I fail, please lift me up and restore me,
so that I can praise your name for ever.
Amen.

33
Joshua

The LORD said to Moses, 'Go up this mountain of the Abarim range, and see the land that I have given to the Israelites. When you have seen it, you also shall be gathered to your people, as your brother Aaron was, because you rebelled against my word in the wilderness of Zin when the congregation quarrelled with me. You did not show my holiness before their eyes at the waters.' (These are the waters of Meribath-kadesh in the wilderness of Zin.) Moses spoke to the LORD, saying, 'Let the LORD, the God of the spirits of all flesh, appoint someone over the congregation who shall go out before them and come in before them, who shall lead them out and bring them in, so that the congregation of the LORD may not be like sheep without a shepherd.' So the LORD said to Moses, 'Take Joshua son of Nun, a man in whom is the spirit, and lay your hand upon him; have him stand before Eleazar the priest and all the congregation, and commission him in their sight. You shall give him some of your authority, so that all the congregation of the Israelites may obey.'
(Numbers 27:12–20)

So again Jesus said to them, 'Very truly, I tell you, I am the gate for the sheep. All who came before me are thieves and bandits; but the sheep did not listen to them. I am the gate. Whoever enters by me will be saved, and will come in and go out and find pasture. The thief comes only to steal and kill and destroy. I came that they may have life, and have it abundantly.

'I am the good shepherd. The good shepherd lays down his life for the sheep.'
(John 10:7–11)

There have been times recently when I have been desperate to *go out*. Having contracted Covid shortly after Christmas 2021, I found myself in isolation and stuck inside. Although I might have been safe inside, as we all were during the various lockdowns that 2020 saw introduced, I was not free. Likewise, in those lockdowns, although folk were protected from contracting the virus, we were not able to go out and find pasture. For some of us, this was more challenging than it was for others. Inside there might be safety, but outside there is pasture and growth.

When Moses faces the task of appointing a successor, he knows that, for God's people to succeed, they will need to come in and go out. Figuratively, this means coming into safety and going out into growth and expansion. Moses, who has spent formative years as a shepherd, knows that sheep will not do this twofold action unaided. It is no different for us. People need a pastor who will open the gate to let them out into liberty and growth, but who will also close the gate behind them, keeping them safe from straying and safe from wolves.

As the story of God's people unfolds over the coming chapters and into the subsequent books of the Hebrew Bible, we will see Joshua fulfil this challenge; he will serve as shepherd of God's people. The English word *pastor*, which we use to refer to the shepherd of people, is the Latin word for 'shepherd' – used for both sheep and humans. It is, in turn, derived from a word which means 'to lead to pasture'. Joshua needs to do this for God's people. When Jesus comes, he tells us that he is the good shepherd. This indicates that he is taking upon himself the mantle of Joshua, but it means so much more. As well as being the one who will lead in and out and bring to pasture, as Joshua was to do, Jesus tells us that he himself is the very gate of the sheep pen through which his flock must go.

As we seek to find both safety and liberty in this wilderness journey of ours, Jesus is our shepherd-guide, leading us in and out and to pasture. What is truly incredible, however, is that, as he shepherds us into safety, it is into himself that he draws us. As the old hymn says: 'Rock of Ages, cleft for me; / let me hide myself in thee.'[1] Safer than any house, or sheep pen, or lockdown, is the merciful heart of Christ where God the Father sees us as one with Jesus. Moreover, as he leads us out to feed us, he does so by sharing himself with us, feeding us with himself so that he is truly born in us.

If you find yourself locked in and unable to go out, let me encourage you to make the most of the time by venturing deeper with Christ, feeding on him through his word.

---

1   A. Toplady, 'Rock of Ages' (1776).

For reflection

- How were you affected by lockdowns and isolation?
- Where might we find pasture with Jesus?

Prayer

Lord Jesus Christ,
We thank you because you have shown yourself
to be the gate of the sheepfold.
Give us the gift of your Spirit
so that we may be led by you
as we come in and go out and find pasture.
Amen.

34
Offerings

At the beginnings of your months you shall offer a burnt-offering to the LORD: two young bulls, one ram, seven male lambs a year old without blemish; also three-tenths of an ephah of choice flour for a grain-offering, mixed with oil, for each bull; and two-tenths of choice flour for a grain-offering, mixed with oil, for the one ram; and one-tenth of choice flour mixed with oil as a grain-offering for every lamb—a burnt-offering of pleasing odour, an offering by fire to the LORD. Their drink-offerings shall be half a hin of wine for a bull, one-third of a hin for a ram, and one-fourth of a hin for a lamb. This is the burnt-offering of every month throughout the months of the year. And there shall be one male goat for a sin-offering to the LORD; it shall be offered in addition to the regular burnt-offering and its drink-offering.
(Numbers 28:11–15)

I appeal to you therefore, brothers and sisters, by the mercies of God, to present your bodies as a living sacrifice, holy and acceptable to God, which is your spiritual worship. Do not be conformed to this world, but be transformed by the renewing of your minds, so that you may discern what is the will of God—what is good and acceptable and perfect.

For by the grace given to me I say to everyone among you not to think of yourself more highly than you ought to think, but to think with sober judgement, each according to the measure of faith that God has assigned.
(Romans 12:1–3)

Our reading from Numbers today steps outside the run of narrative, which has been flowing along drawing God's people towards the promised land. It does so in order for us to hear some commands of God to his people.

Arguably, these commands are not aspects of the universal moral law in the same way that the Ten Commandments or the laws given to Noah were. They would not, therefore, be immediately binding on us as Gentile believers. They are not to be discarded, however.

They are recorded for us to learn from. Instead of receiving them as rituals for us to follow in our various churches, we are to understand them as ceremonial provisions given, in line with the moral law, so that God's people living under the old covenant could know they were worshipping God in a way that pleased him. In order to please God, his people must have faith. God asks the Israelites to demonstrate this faith in the sacrifice or giving up of valuable consumable goods such as grains, oil, meat and so on.

Although each offering may have a particular symbolic relevance,[1] the purpose of sacrifice more generally is threefold. First, sacrifice shows that the worshipper acknowledges and thanks God for having provided the items being sacrificed; second, sacrifice shows that the worshipper values God more than they value the items being sacrificed; and finally, sacrifice shows that the worshipper trusts God to continue to provide for them. This is, in a sense, a threefold definition of faith: thankfulness for the past, value for the present and trust for the future.

The Israelites in the wilderness were given the command to offer various sacrifices which in the wilderness they could not fulfil. This is to show that joined to the command is a promise: as God commands, so he provides. God demands from us that which he alone can enable us to offer. God does not require material sacrifices from us in our wilderness, but sacrifice is still the lived expression of our faith.

When we make sacrifices, by elevating our service of God above the lesser goods of this world, we live out our faith. We live out our thankfulness for all that God has given us, we live out the value we place in God, and we live out the trust we have that he will continue to provide for us.

Christianity is a sacrificial religion; God asks a lot from us. He asks for our very lives. He asks more than we could naturally give, as he asked of the Israelites in the wilderness. Crucially, however, as he asks so he provides. As he once asked for grain and oil and followed this with a promise to provide those things, now he asks for our life in joyful service,

---

1 See G. Wenham, *Numbers,* Tyndale Old Testament Commentaries 4 (Nottingham: Inter-Varsity Press, 2008), for more information on the symbolic nature of sacrifices.

linking this to a promise for life abundant and the power of the Spirit to do all that he has asked.

For reflection
- What have you sacrificed for God, and what might he be asking you to sacrifice next?
- How do our little sacrifices add to the glory of Jesus' full and final sacrifice?

Prayer
Merciful God,
anything you require from us you have already given us;
help us joyfully to lay down all that you have placed in our hands,
as we are remade in the image of your Son,
who laid down his glory, that he might make a final sacrifice for sin.
Amen.

Part 6

THE JOURNEY'S END (NUMBERS 31:1 – 36:13)

We have made it to our final week of journeying through the wilderness with God's people. We have ahead of us some of the most difficult and challenging terrain to cover, as we encounter divinely mandated war, the destruction of idols, and the urge to abandon the journey for some pleasant strip of wilderness. But if we push through, we will find our wilderness journey furnished with new insights and equipped with new strengths.

Holy Week

Monday: war (Numbers 31:1–8)
Tuesday: settling (Numbers 32:1–6)
Wednesday: idols (Numbers 33:50–5)
Thursday: refuge (Numbers 35:9–15)
Friday: blood (Numbers 35:30–3)
Saturday: inheritance (Numbers 36:5–9)

35

War

The LORD spoke to Moses, saying, 'Avenge the Israelites on the Midianites; afterwards you shall be gathered to your people.' So Moses said to the people, 'Arm some of your number for the war, so that they may go against Midian, to execute the LORD's vengeance on Midian. You shall send a thousand from each of the tribes of Israel to the war.' So out of the thousands of Israel, a thousand from each tribe were conscripted, twelve thousand armed for battle. Moses sent them to the war, a thousand from each tribe, along with Phinehas son of Eleazar the priest, with the vessels of the sanctuary and the trumpets for sounding the alarm in his hand. They did battle against Midian, as the LORD had commanded Moses, and killed every male. They killed the kings of Midian: Evi, Rekem, Zur, Hur, and Reba, the five kings of Midian, in addition to others who were slain by them; and they also killed Balaam son of Beor with the sword.

(Numbers 31:1–8)

While he was still speaking, Judas, one of the twelve, arrived; with him was a large crowd with swords and clubs, from the chief priests and the elders of the people. Now the betrayer had given them a sign, saying, 'The one I will kiss is the man; arrest him.' At once he came up to Jesus and said, 'Greetings, Rabbi!' and kissed him. Jesus said to him, 'Friend, do what you are here to do.' Then they came and laid hands on Jesus and arrested him. Suddenly, one of those with Jesus put his hand on his sword, drew it, and struck the slave of the high priest, cutting off his ear. Then Jesus said to him, 'Put your sword back into its place; for all who take the sword will perish by the sword.'

(Matthew 26:47–52)

'War is hell', is the oft repeated phrase, which finds its way on to the lips of Harry Welsh in the HBO drama, *Band of Brothers*.[1] Set during the Second World War, this series gives a glimpse into some of the traumas and tragedies of warfare. We don't have to look hard at the Bible to find war and human conflict. Sometimes, especially in the Old Testament, we find stories about war which involved a divine command.

There is much that can be said, and has been said in other places, about how best to interpret and apply such passages. They seem, at first glance, to be so far away from the God of love whom we have come to know through Jesus Christ – or, indeed, in many other passages of the Old Testament. But it is worse than naïve simply to write off these accounts as fragments of Bronze Age blood lust. Instead, we must work hard to understand how these aspects of the Israelite's wilderness journey sustained them through later years, both while they were living in the promised land and during their subsequent exile. We must also understand that these stories form part of the same Scripture that the New Testament tells us will 'instruct you for salvation through faith in Christ Jesus' (2 Timothy 3:15).

In Israel's wilderness journey, war is the means of enacting God's plan, but it also acts as a mirror for later events in the story of God's people. There, once we reach the books of the Prophets, we see pagan nations raised up against Israel for the same ultimate purpose as the Israelites were raised up in Numbers. What we learn, in time, is that God is the God of the whole world, working invisibly – at times imperceptibly – in every nation. And, moreover, God enacts his purposes with whatever tools he chooses.

Likewise, the wars which we read about in the opening books of the Bible are earthly and temporal means of securing the earthly and temporal promises of God. The people of God are now a spiritual people, drawn from every tribe and tongue, looking for a spiritual fulfilment of the promised land. We strive for these promises by spiritual means. But we know to strive, and understand the life-and-death significance of our struggle, because of the stories of God's people having to wage war to secure their promises.

The promises to which we aspire are spiritual, and the wilderness in which we await those promises is spiritual too. In this way, we learn that

---

1 T. Hanks and S. Spielberg (prod.), *Band of Brothers: Part 2: War Is Hell* (2001).

our enemy is not human, nor can it be conquered by force. We must wage a spiritual war against our threefold spiritual enemy: sin, the world and the devil. It will require us to muster all our strength but, instead of going to war to attain personal ends with violence, we must surrender in loving service to God. For it is God, in Jesus Christ, who has overcome.

For reflection

- It is said that 'war is hell'. Do you know anyone who has had first-hand experience of war? How did it affect them?
- How are we to wage a spiritual war against the forces of evil?

Prayer

Father, you are the God of peace;
hasten the day when wars will cease in all the world,
and when all will be your love, glory and righteousness.
Give us the grace to fight courageously against the spiritual powers of darkness,
and the compassion always to care for our brothers and sisters.
Amen.

36
Settling

Now the Reubenites and the Gadites owned a very great number of cattle. When they saw that the land of Jazer and the land of Gilead was a good place for cattle, the Gadites and the Reubenites came and spoke to Moses, to Eleazar the priest, and to the leaders of the congregation, saying, 'Ataroth, Dibon, Jazer, Nimrah, Heshbon, Elealeh, Sebam, Nebo, and Beon— the land that the Lord subdued before the congregation of Israel—is a land for cattle; and your servants have cattle.' They continued, 'If we have found favour in your sight, let this land be given to your servants for a possession; do not make us cross the Jordan.'

But Moses said to the Gadites and to the Reubenites, 'Shall your brothers go to war while you sit here?'
(Numbers 32:1–6)

As they were going along the road, someone said to him, 'I will follow you wherever you go.' And Jesus said to him, 'Foxes have holes, and birds of the air have nests; but the Son of Man has nowhere to lay his head.' To another he said, 'Follow me.' But he said, 'Lord, first let me go and bury my father.' But Jesus said to him, 'Let the dead bury their own dead; but as for you, go and proclaim the kingdom of God.' Another said, 'I will follow you, Lord; but let me first say farewell to those at my home.' Jesus said to him, 'No one who puts a hand to the plough and looks back is fit for the kingdom of God.'
(Luke 9:57–62)

It can be very easy to stop. I have found it much easier to stop short than to finish. I wonder if you have had the same experience. I have lost count of the number of times when, running a course, I have felt too tired and stopped, ashamed by how close I was to the finish before stopping. I won't mention the urge to stop writing these devotions now that we are in the final week. In our reading from Numbers today, the Reubenites and the Gadites, two of the twelve tribes of Israel, stop short.

Awed by the pleasantness and fecundity of Gilead, some of God's people abandon their inheritance beyond the River Jordan in the promised land. They give up on the promise of land, wanting to settle instead for the most pleasant slice of wilderness that they have so far discovered. This can be a trap for us, too. As we journey through our spiritual wilderness, there will be oases of rest and refreshment; there will be spiritual Gileads. These will be places that we find to be good, places of ease, where we are not too greatly challenged. We will want to stop our spiritual journey there. It will seem like enough. But it is not.

Although, graciously, Moses permits the Reubenites and Gadites to forfeit their inheritance and share of the promised land, in exchange for pasture in Gilead and Jazer, nevertheless they must first still cross the Jordan and take possession of the promised land with the whole of God's people. There will be times in our spiritual Gileads when we will need to hear the words of Moses, 'Shall your brothers go to war while you sit here?'

Perhaps we have a comfortable job, enabling us comfortably to tithe to a comfortable church. 'It is good here!' we might cry. It may well be comfortable, but as the late Pope Benedict XVI has been misquoted as saying, 'The world offers you comfort. But you were not made for comfort. You were made for greatness.'[1] The greatness for which we were made is the greatness that comes from conformity to, or growing in likeness to, Jesus. It is a greatness which we know, paradoxically, only in weakness as we journey through this wilderness life.

As we press on towards the Jordan, we must keep Jesus fixed in our minds as our pattern of life. He must always be our model, calling us on to new challenges as long as we live. He did not settle in the Gilead of life, with a comfortable teaching ministry. He despised the shame, and endured death, even death on the cross. We must not stop; the promised land will be greater than Gilead.

---

1 The closest we come to this powerful phrase in the teaching of Benedict was in an encyclical: 'The ways of the Lord are not easy, but we were not created for an easy life, but for great things, for goodness.' Pope Benedict XVI, *Spe salvi*, section 33.

For reflection

- Have you ever stopped short of all that God was calling you to, because it was more comfortable to stay where you were?
- What does it mean to be made for greatness?

Prayer

Lord Jesus, keep us faithful to your calling,
and give us the grace to persevere to the end,
that with all your saints in glory,
we may obtain our eternal inheritance.
Amen.

37

Idols

In the plains of Moab by the Jordan at Jericho, the LORD spoke to Moses, saying: Speak to the Israelites, and say to them: When you cross over the Jordan into the land of Canaan, you shall drive out all the inhabitants of the land from before you, destroy all their figured stones, destroy all their cast images, and demolish all their high places. You shall take possession of the land and settle in it, for I have given you the land to possess. You shall apportion the land by lot according to your clans; to a large one you shall give a large inheritance, and to a small one you shall give a small inheritance; the inheritance shall belong to the person on whom the lot falls; according to your ancestral tribes you shall inherit. But if you do not drive out the inhabitants of the land from before you, then those whom you let remain shall be as barbs in your eyes and thorns in your sides; they shall trouble you in the land where you are settling. (Numbers 33:50–5)

When Christ who is your life is revealed, then you also will be revealed with him in glory.
    Put to death, therefore, whatever in you is earthly: fornication, impurity, passion, evil desire, and greed (which is idolatry). On account of these the wrath of God is coming on those who are disobedient.
(Colossians 3:4–6)

There is to be no idolatry in the promised land. Indeed, idolatry would rob the promised land of its glory, glory which should subsist in providing a context for unimpaired worship of God, for it is God's glory to which all good things must point. Idolatry, at its most basic, is the love of a gift that spurns the giver. God is the giver of all good gifts, and we must be cautious not to love the gifts he gives in a way which neglects him. We can easily think of the excited child on Christmas morning, so frantically opening his presents that he doesn't even notice the tag which would tell him from whom the gift has come. As we grow, we should learn that this joy in reception must itself grow into gratitude and affection for the one who gave the gift.

The idolatry we encounter in Numbers goes beyond this simple definition. Here we see people who have not only spurned the giver of gifts, but have elevated to divine status the gifts themselves. They have robbed God of the glory which should have been owed him through the good things of this world, offering it instead to fictions and fantasies contrived by their own imagination and constructed by their own hands. If God's people are going to be able to live in peace, fully giving themselves to God in lives of worship, there can be no trace of idolatry in their midst.

What we discover, as we make our way through the grand sweep of Old Testament narrative, is that God's people never succeed in ridding their promised land of idolatry. It remains a snare to them. Again and again, they lose sight of their faith and follow pagan nations down blind alleys and spiritual cul-de-sacs. From this, we can identify the ways in which this wilderness life will be beset by idolatry. We will not escape it entirely, and so we must be conscious of its threat and tear down every idol that our heart puts up, smashing every altar in our heart on which we offer sacrifices to anyone except the Lord.

Greed, says the New Testament, is idolatry. Perhaps this is one of the most basic applications of what we have learned from today's Numbers passage: as we survey our hearts, if we find greed – the desire to hoard for ourselves rather than employing wealth for the glory of God – we are guilty of idolatry. We, like the Israelites, must find a way to enjoy our inheritance in the promised land, and the tokens of that promise which we receive in God's good blessings, in a way that increases his glory rather than diminishing it.

For reflection
- What things, good or bad, have you made idols out of?
- Do you believe yourself to be a greedy person?

Prayer
Loving Father, who made us in your image,
to reflect your goodness and beauty,

give us the power of your Holy Spirit
and enable us to tear down the idols of our heart,
so that we can be remade
in the image of your Son.
Amen.

38
Refuge

The LORD spoke to Moses, saying: Speak to the Israelites, and say to them: When you cross the Jordan into the land of Canaan, then you shall select cities to be cities of refuge for you, so that a slayer who kills a person without intent may flee there. The cities shall be for you a refuge from the avenger, so that the slayer may not die until there is a trial before the congregation. The cities that you designate shall be six cities of refuge for you: you shall designate three cities beyond the Jordan, and three cities in the land of Canaan, to be cities of refuge. These six cities shall serve as refuge for the Israelites, for the resident or transient alien among them, so that anyone who kills a person without intent may flee there.

(Numbers 35:9–15)

'Do not let your hearts be troubled. Believe in God, believe also in me. In my Father's house there are many dwelling-places. If it were not so, would I have told you that I go to prepare a place for you? And if I go and prepare a place for you, I will come again and will take you to myself, so that where I am, there you may be also. And you know the way to the place where I am going.' Thomas said to him, 'Lord, we do not know where you are going. How can we know the way?' Jesus said to him, 'I am the way, and the truth, and the life. No one comes to the Father except through me.'

(John 14:1–6)

Where do you feel safest? The 2002 thriller, *Panic Room*, introduced audiences to the idea of a safe vault within a house, where family members could hide in the event of a home invasion or burglary – the eponymous panic room. As the film played out, viewers could question just how safe it really was. Feeling safe, for me, isn't always about where I am geographically. It isn't always about place, but rather it is to do with people.

I feel safest when I am around those who I trust the most, especially in those situations where I am able to rely on them. For this reason, I feel safe afloat on the lifeboat here in Porthcawl. Not because I am naïve to the risks – but because I trust the helm and the crew, and so I can take refuge from my fears in their skills.

In the wilderness, there are few places of safety and few places of refuge. Whether beset by natural disasters, the anger of other travellers, or the wrath of God working itself out through either of these, God's people in the wilderness find themselves in desperate need of a refuge. The promised land is to be that earthly refuge. Accordingly, as God prepares his people to take hold of the promised land, he also instructs them to designate places, cities or towns, to be places of particular refuge. These are to be places where people can go to be safe. Places where people can escape the wrath of those who they have unintentionally wronged, provided they know the way.

In our spiritual wilderness journey, we make our way towards our spiritual promised land. This will not merely have half a dozen cities of refuge within it, but will itself be an eternal refuge. Once there, we will be safe for ever. We can know that safety, that refuge, even now in this life. We can know it by faith, because the safety that we are afforded in the world to come is the same salvation that Christ offers us now. As we come to him, he shields us from the dangers of this world, but also keeps us safe from the wrath which is to come, as 1 Thessalonians 1:10 says.

Christ is our safe refuge. When we are in danger, we can flee to him. He will shield us within his merciful heart, and carry us safely all the days of our life that we belong to him. He guides us through the dangers of this wilderness, through the passage of death, through the day of judgement, and for ever.

For reflection

- Where do you feel safest and why?
- Is the Church a place where you feel safe? If not, why not?

Prayer

Lead me, O Lord, in your righteousness
because of my enemies;
make your way straight before me.

But let all who take refuge in you rejoice;
let them ever sing for joy.
Spread your protection over them,
so that those who love your name may exult in you.
For you bless the righteous, O Lord;
you cover them with favour as with a shield.
Amen.

39
Blood

If anyone kills another, the murderer shall be put to death on the evidence of witnesses; but no one shall be put to death on the testimony of a single witness. Moreover, you shall accept no ransom for the life of a murderer who is subject to the death penalty; a murderer must be put to death. Nor shall you accept ransom for one who has fled to a city of refuge, enabling the fugitive to return to live in the land before the death of the high priest. You shall not pollute the land in which you live; for blood pollutes the land, and no expiation can be made for the land, for the blood that is shed in it, except by the blood of the one who shed it.
(Numbers 35:30–3)

For if the blood of goats and bulls, with the sprinkling of the ashes of a heifer, sanctifies those who have been defiled so that their flesh is purified, how much more will the blood of Christ, who through the eternal Spirit offered himself without blemish to God, purify our conscience from dead works to worship the living God!

For this reason he is the mediator of a new covenant, so that those who are called may receive the promised eternal inheritance, because a death has occurred that redeems them from the transgressions under the first covenant.
(Hebrews 9:13–15)

Blood is powerful stuff. From a physical perspective, it transports oxygen to the cells of the body, as well as removing the waste carbon dioxide. It also carries the nutrients and hormones our cells need and holds the white blood cells that are needed to fight infections. With the illumination of modern science, it can be easy to understand why Leviticus 17:14 says, 'The life of every creature is its blood.' The authors of the Old Testament understood the significance of blood, but they see further than we might do through a microscope.

As part of the ritual cleansing of the sins of Israel, Aaron, the high priest of Israel, must offer blood. An animal's unblemished life, its blood, is used sacramentally to wash away the sins of the people. Sadly for the animal in question, the only way to get at the life is for it to die.

In the cosmic-spiritual accounting of the Old Testament, most sins can be remedied by the sacrifice of an animal – but not the murder of a human. Human blood cannot be weighed in the scales with anything less vital or valuable. Innocent blood is said to cry out for vengeance when it has been unjustly shed, as in the story of Cain and Abel. In our reading from Numbers today, we see shed blood polluting the land. The language here almost has overtones of environmental pollution. We have come to understand the moral connotations of environmental disasters, so perhaps we can understand such pollution by picturing an oil spill.[1] Letting a murder like this pass without taking action points to a moral or spiritual crisis within the community, a spiritual injustice or debt that must be remedied.

The solution given in Numbers is straightforward enough and is consonant with the recurrent laws of retribution: an eye for an eye, or here blood for blood. The reality is that the blood of bulls and goats can never really purify us. Not from murder, but also not from any of the various sins we commit. But in and through the significance of blood as a sacramental sign, we find a message about Jesus Christ. His life of perfect obedience, even obedience unto death upon the cross, allowed him to be presented as truly spotless and willing. In pouring out his blood, he washes us clean and redeems us in a cosmic double exchange: my sins are imputed to him on the cross, and his obedience is imputed to me before the throne of judgement.

Upon the cross, Jesus offers up his life, his blood, to cleanse us from every stain of sin – his perfect life, his obedience to the law, his living out of the love that the Father wishes us all to share, poured out upon the altar of the cross.

For reflection

- What is the significance of Jesus' blood?
- How can the Church honour more clearly what the Bible teaches about blood?

---

1 For more on the spiritual dimension of environmental issues, see R. J. Berry and L. Yoder, *John Stott on Creation Care* (London: IVP, 2021).

Prayer

Lord Jesus Christ,
help me to know the power of your blood;
may it cleanse me and heal me,
as I am washed through by it.
Amen.

40

Inheritance

Then Moses commanded the Israelites according to the word of the
LORD, saying, 'The descendants of the tribe of Joseph are right in
what they are saying. This is what the LORD commands concerning
the daughters of Zelophehad, "Let them marry whom they think
best; only it must be into a clan of their father's tribe that they are
married, so that no inheritance of the Israelites shall be transferred
from one tribe to another; for all Israelites shall retain the inheritance
of their ancestral tribes. Every daughter who possesses an inheritance
in any tribe of the Israelites shall marry one from the clan of her
father's tribe, so that all Israelites may continue to possess their
ancestral inheritance. No inheritance shall be transferred from one
tribe to another; for each of the tribes of the Israelites shall retain its
own inheritance."'
(Numbers 36:5–9)

In Christ we have also obtained an inheritance, having been
destined according to the purpose of him who accomplishes all
things according to his counsel and will, so that we, who were the
first to set our hope on Christ, might live for the praise of his glory.
In him you also, when you had heard the word of truth, the gospel
of your salvation, and had believed in him, were marked with the
seal of the promised Holy Spirit; this is the pledge of our inheritance
toward redemption as God's own people, to the praise of his glory.
(Ephesians 1:11–14)

We have made it to the last day of our wandering through the wilderness
with God's people, and here we pause with them to reflect on the
inheritance that is ahead of us. For the ancient Israelites, there was an
earthly and temporal inheritance of land waiting for them at the end
of their journey. This was to be a place to live, a refuge and the means of

securing many blessings. These were the blessing of freedom from slavery, of peace from oppression and war, of possession of all that was needed to live good and abundant lives on earth; but, most significantly, the blessing that would come from living as the people of God with God in their midst. This inheritance was to be held inviolable by clans, so that it could not be hoarded by a wealthy elite to the exclusion of the poor or dispossessed. It was to be an inheritance passed from generation to generation, with both men and women benefiting from it.

There is little evidence to suggest that the inheritance of land was ever, let alone always, treated with the reverence which its status as the means of mediating God's blessing deserved. If we read on through the pages of the Old Testament, we discover kings who wrongfully take land at the expense of others, we find the poor left uncared for – in short, we find the inheritance disregarded and abused.

For us, in our wilderness journey, we do not look to a merely earthly or temporal inheritance. The inheritance that we look to is ultimately spiritual, and it is imperishable, secured for ever in heaven because our promised land lies beyond this life, when we are raised to eternal life with Jesus. This means that our spiritual wandering is not limited to forty years in the wilderness, but it is lifelong. We will not, in this life, take full possession of our inheritance. Nevertheless, God in his mercy and love does give us a foretaste of his heavenly banquet – a pledge or deposit towards our inheritance. This taster of God's rule is to be shared and enjoyed by all God's people as life on earth is brought into alignment with God's kingdom – with justice, righteousness and provision.

Before I trained to be a vicar, I used to work in property law. When a person looks to buy a house, they will secure the deal with a down payment or deposit. This part payment does more than simply pay off a fraction of the asking price – it acts as a sort of guarantee against the whole sum. Although of course it doesn't always work like this, the idea is that, when a person puts down a deposit, we can be sure they will follow through with the full amount.

We do not yet have possession of all that God has in store for us, but if we put our trust in Jesus, we do have the deposit of the Holy Spirit given to us as a pledge. This forms the first part of our inheritance – God's dwelling with us. But it also assures us that God truly has bought us with the blood of Christ. It assures us that we do have an inheritance waiting for us when, on the day when we breathe our last, we will pass from this wilderness journey into our promised land.

For reflection

- What is the inheritance stored up for us in heaven?
- How can we live our earthly lives in a way that is worthy of the heavenly promised land?

Prayer

Father,
in your love you guide us all the days of our life,
through wilderness and through pleasant places.
Give us grace so that we can learn to know your presence
in joys and in sorrows,
and so become ready to take hold of all that you have promised
through your Son, Jesus Christ Our Lord.
Amen.

Epilogue to the travelogue

Thank you for journeying with me this Lent.

During the last forty days, we have trod the path of God's people in the wilderness through the book of Numbers. This Old Testament book, read alongside scriptures from the New Testament, has given us the opportunity to reflect on the ways in which we can know God better, and recognise his presence and promise throughout our lives. By learning from these often difficult passages, we can see the Lord at work in our wanderings – even in the hard times. In our travels and in our travails, in our journeying and when facing our Jordans, God has promised to be with us by his Spirit when we put our trust in his Son. God being with us changes everything. Even when the circumstances around us won't change, we find that we are changed within them.

Our time on earth will not always consist of wilderness wanderings. Sometimes, it will feel as though we are trapped in a wilderness, sentenced to remain there all our days. People who have been bereaved, or who have suffered a difficult relationship breakdown, may know this feeling. Looking to the horizon and seeing only dust can make it hard to have hope that there is an oasis just beyond.

When I preach on Psalm 23 at funerals, I sometimes try to challenge this perspective. Looking at the promises given to the believer in this psalm, we see blessings for both here and hereafter. Accordingly, at a funeral, it can help to encourage people to enjoy the good things that God provides in this life, while always looking for the good things of the life to come. It is my experience that the presence of God, his abiding peace and power, is the greatest gift that we can receive in this life. Experiencing it draws our eyes across the Jordan to the fullness of his presence that we will enjoy after we are raised to life. The good things that God provides in this life do not mean that we will never encounter the wilderness, but they do assure us that we do not have to cross it alone or unprepared.

My prayer is that, in the days and years to come, you will continue to travel with God. If your life is typical, your journey will see you go through pleasant valleys as well as tracks of dry wilderness – regardless of which,

God's offer to travel with you is firm. Open his word, hear him speak and allow him to orientate you, whatever your surroundings. As you continue on your journey, you may want to travel deeper into the book of Numbers. If this sort of study is new to you, then you can do no better than to read Gordon Wenham's Tyndale Old Testament Commentary or Raymond Brown's Bible Speaks Today volume (for full details, see the Further reading that follows).

Further reading

On Numbers

Brown, Raymond, *The Message of Numbers*, The Bible Speaks Today (London: IVP, 2021).

Olson, Dennis T., *Numbers: Interpretation: A Bible commentary for preaching and teaching* (Louisville, KY: Presbyterian Publishing, 2014).

Stubbs, David L., *Numbers*, SCM Theological Commentary on the Bible (London: SCM Press, 2009).

Wenham, Gordon, *Numbers*, Tyndale Old Testament Commentary (Nottingham: IVP, 2008).

For in-depth study of the Old Testament texts

Ashley, Timothy R., *The Book of Numbers*, 2nd edn, New International Commentary on the Old Testament (Grand Rapids, MI: Eerdmans, 2022).

Briggs, Richard S., *Theological Hermeneutics and the Book of Numbers as Christian Scripture* (Notre Dame, IN: University of Notre Dame Press, 2018).

Wright, Christopher, *Old Testament Ethics for the People of God* (Nottingham: IVP, 2010).

Other forty-day devotionals

Clarke, Ros, *Forty Women: Unseen women of the Bible* (London: IVP, 2021).

Gatiss, Lee, et al., *Foundations of Faith: Reflections on the 39 Articles* (London: Church Society/Lost Coin, 2019).

Stott, John and Wright, Chris, *The Radical Reconciler: Lent in all the Scriptures* (London: IVP, 2019).